I Heart Creativity

I Heart Creativity

A Guide to Defining Your Creative Purpose and Anchoring Yourself in Change

Courtney Feider

ISBN-13: 9781548249168
ISBN-10: 1548249165

TABLE OF CONTENTS

Foreword by Jeff Reynolds · xv
Introduction by Justin Foster · xix

Chapter 1   I Heart Creativity ·1
Chapter 2   How Did We Get Here? ·9
Chapter 3   The Genius of the Creative Heart · · · · · · · · · · · · · · ·17
Chapter 4   The Unique You ·27
Chapter 5   How You Got Lost ·39
Chapter 6   Who Hurt You? ·45
Chapter 7   Finding Your Creative Nature · · · · · · · · · · · · · · · · · ·57
Chapter 8   Defining Creative Leadership · · · · · · · · · · · · · · · · · ·67
Chapter 9   Your Creative Type ·73
Chapter 10   Creative Support vs. Creative Prohibition · · · · · · · · · · ·85
Chapter 11   Changing Your World ·91
Chapter 12   Conclusions ·99

For the People I Love ·105
About The Author ·109
Working with Courtney · 111

"I'll be the Earth to ground you
From the chaos all around
I'll be the home you return to
I can be your middle ground
And I will serve as a reminder
If you jump you will not fall
Go on and spread those wings of reason
We are water after all

You can trust me in my instincts
'Cause they are like that of a bird
I am loyal, I will feed you
And sing you songs you never heard
Who wants to wear the hat this morning
I reckon neither of us cares
Cause there is more to life than leading
And I would follow you I swear

And if you call on me
I'll come running like a coyote
Cause we're pillars indeed
A lighthouse when you're out to sea
A beacon when direction is all I need
A compass if you know what I mean
Drunk on that nectar of all that you are to me."

NAHKO BEAR
TUS PIES (YOUR FEET)

PRAISE FOR I HEART CREATIVITY

"*I Heart Creativity* opens the dialogue about creativity, what it means, and how it affects our vulnerability and happiness as well as fundamental business success. It connects us to what we have been through, what we have displaced or neglected in our creative selves, and what we need to do to re-open our creative hearts. As someone who fundamentally overhauled my business at its peak to connect with my truest and most creative self, I believe wholeheartedly in this message and its importance for each and every person."

JASON ZOOK
Entrepreneur
Jason Does Stuff

"Courtney has offered us a roadmap to creative leadership, for ourselves and the people we lead. Creativity is needed more than ever in these disruptive and exponentially changing times we are living in."

TOM HOOD, CPA, CITP, CGMA
CEO of the Business Learning Institute and
Maryland Association of CPAs

"Courtney Feider gives us permission to explore what we are passionate about. I wouldn't have had the confidence to do these things and put myself on the path that I am currently on without *I Heart Creativity* and Courtney's work."

TSCHARNER HUNTER, MBA
Dartmouth College
Tuck School of Business, Class of 2017

"*I Heart Creativity* has thoughtful frameworks, brought to life by vulnerable, real stories. Courtney inspires and challenges us to use creativity to live with purpose and meaning."

JESSICA ROLPH
Founder / Board Member
Happy Family Brands

"The key phrase from this stellar book is this: 'When we do wake up, we will see that what lies in the center of nearly every modern dilemma is a creative heart.' This is where every leader finds themselves today - at the yes/no moment of deciding to organize a life or business around this creative heart. If you're answer is not yet a hearty 'yes', this book will give you the courage to do so."

JUSTIN FOSTER
Founder
Root & River

"Courtney writes with fiery eloquence and surgical incisiveness about the creativity engineered into our hearts, which we can choose to suppress or to actualize. She shows us how to release the power of creativity in our life and work starting with the choice to be authentically ourselves, and to be counter-intuitively vulnerable in our interactions. What she describes can unleash transformative processes that bring us finally to our true selves. She challenges us to embrace the potential of creative disruption personally, laying out a pragmatic methodology for self assessment and for action. This is a wonderful, philosophically nuanced, frequently meditative and evidence-based work that should be widely read."

DEV RAMCHARAN, PMPP, CCTC
Portfolio Director, Governance, DMO, ITS Strategic Initiatives and CTB Delivery
TD Bank

"Courtney has made the case for disrupting corporate cultures by introducing creativity into everyday life. Her stories and practical tips will change your way of looking at self and your world to produce greater result for your organization and happiness for the reader."

WHIT MITCHELL
Founder
Working in Sync

"Not only will this book help reawaken you to your creativity and its importance, this book will change you. The world is waiting for you to discover and offer your unique gifts. This book will help you find and share them. Those fortunate enough to work with Courtney know the power of her message and her methods—and the incredible heart she brings to her work. She is creativity embodied."

LISA FISHER
Leadership and Organizational Development Strategist
Consultant & Executive Coach
Author of Admissions by Design

"We're all born creative. Then, life happens. For various reasons, many of us get disconnected from our creative self. Courtney's book, *I Heart Creativity*, helps us understand how that may have happened, how to get back in touch with this deep part of ourselves, and why getting reconnected is so critical for our own success and the overall effectiveness of the organizations in which we lead and serve. If you're not convinced of the value and need for creativity as a key advantage in the workplace, you need to read this book and see what you think after hearing Courtney's persuasive arguments. This is a great addition to the literature on creativity. I highly recommend this book to people who want to find their best self and do their best and most creative work."

ANDY JOHNSON
Executive Coach / Team Health Specialist
Author of Introvert Revolution

"At long last someone has delivered what creative people who happen to also be business people have been seeking -- a full look at the power and genius of creative energy and how to tap into it and a guide for how to tap into it.

She even gathers those of us who find ourselves a bit lost on our way to creativity and maps a road back. Well-researched, insightful, inspiring and above all, actionable, I recommend Courtney's personal and passionate plea for the return to our creative power."

EMILY SOCCORSY
Founder - EmJoy, Inc.
Co-Founder - Root & River

"Courtney Feider observes, measures, plans out and then scales Creativity as if it is her own personal mountain. In conquering her own creativity, Courtney then pragmatically outlines it for you and me. She breathes in the scope of Creativity and systematically explains it to us from the top down. In *I Heart Creativity*, we learn how to identify, approach and harness our creative selves to implement this precious gift that may be currently hidden. Courtney uses a series of questions throughout the book, and she has generated a powerful creative diagnostic, the Creative Types Survey, for us to use to understand how to approach and apply our own creativity."

MINDY MIREK BORTNESS
Founder
Communication Works, Inc.

"Courtney Feider has interwoven her personal insights and experiences with those of other successful creatives. Her storytelling will inspire reluctant creatives to be courageous and go for it."

DR. LISA ALDISERT
Author of Leadership Reflections

"Courtney has proven once again that she is an independent, creative and practical thinker. She doesn't fit into anyone else's box and when you embrace her unique experiences and knowledge, you are will be enriched. You will want to read and re-read the first few chapters of 'I Heart Creativity' in order to connect with Courtney's heart, which she posits should come before mind. Then, in subsequent chapters, she satisfies our minds with great research, entertaining stories and a clear pathway to embracing and nurturing creativity in our lives, leadership and teams. This book adds valuable content to the subject of creativity and why creativity from the heart is the key to exploring and realizing our potential to become our better selves."

RON PRICE
Founder/CEO
Price Associates

FOREWORD
by JEFF REYNOLDS

Creativity is so often — too often — treated like an innate, fixed talent. You either have it or you don't. You're good at it or you're not.

This is just plain wrong.

Anyone can be creative. Anyone can add value through creativity. And anyone can enhance their own life through creativity. Like any muscle, your creativity must be strengthened, honed and activated to feel its power. It can be done. You can do it. More to the point: you must do it.

Creativity is what separates humans from machines. Heck, each of our unique brands of creativity is what separates us from each other. We all have a responsibility to identify and master our creativity for the betterment of ourselves, our communities and, as dramatic as it may sound, humankind.

Early in my career I tried the machine route. Despite being in a "creative" field, my day-to-day existence was about mimicking my boss. I was young and insecure. Instead of carving my own way, I copied his way. It didn't work. I enjoyed my work, but the tension of not being myself left me unable to sleep and stressed out. Only once I allowed myself to find my own, unique creative center was I able to supercharge my performance. Not surprisingly (now), when I performed better as a developing version of my true creative self instead of a defective carbon copy of my boss.

Today my life revolves around my identification and application of my creative strengths. I live a portfolio life, with 50% of my time spent advising mid- and large-size companies on modern marketing, 50% of my time experimenting in a laboratory of my own small software companies, and 50% coaching startups. Free time (I feel like I have more of it than ever) is spent enjoying downtime with my family or traveling the world.

It's a good life. But one that's only possible because of the changing role of creativity in my work and society at large. Too many people are stuck in industrial revolution-age thinking. Back then, work required relatively few creative-minded inventors to imagine the machines that workers would run on behalf of the investors who owned the equipment, factories and, often, even distribution channels.

For most companies, the "means of production" are no longer expensive land, steel, railroads, and the like. Instead we increasingly rely on know-how, analysis, data, systems, brand, and cheap computers to create value. All of which are either reliant on or made significantly more effective with a healthy dose of creativity.

For the first time in a long time, arguably ever, workers own the primary means of production. You (we!) have everything you (we!) need to create meaningful value for others and capture some portion of that for yourself (ourselves!). But all this opportunity is hard to seize without creativity.

This isn't pie-in-the-sky thinking, either.

Of the top five companies on *Forbes* most recent list of valuable brands — Apple, Google, Microsoft, Coca-Cola and Facebook — all rely on creativity to create value. In most cases, creativity is their core ingredient (Coke being the exception; sugar still rules).

In small business the role of creativity is even more obvious. A study by Intuit estimates more than 40% of the American workforce will be independent workers. That's 60 million people, mostly using their brains, not their fancy equipment-stuffed factories, to earn a living and build wealth. I personally know dozens if not hundreds of these people. I consider myself one them.

Spreadsheets, words and laptops may be our tools, but our base material is creativity.

If you plan on working for us, competing with us, or simply living in the same universe as us, harnessing the drivers and power of your creativity is no longer a want-to-have skill, it's a need-to-have skill.

The framework Courtney provides here is the first step. It will challenge your understanding of yourself and the role creativity plays in your business life, as well as the rest of your life. It will put you on the road to change.

Even if you're one of those people — particularly if you're one of those people — who has been labeled by others or yourself as "not creative," please know that's not true. We all have it. We all use it. Perhaps it's just nascent or buried beneath a crust of self-consciousness.

But it is there… within you.
Read this.
Find it. Build it.
And set it free.

I promise you'll love the results.

JEFF REYNOLDS
Marketing Professional and Creative Entrepreneur
Boise, Idaho (and The World)

INTRODUCTION
by JUSTIN FOSTER

It's always interesting the first lens we look through when we meet some- one new. The first lens I saw Courtney Feider through was her work as an Event Strategist and Producer. I was booked by Courtney to provide a series of personal branding workshops around the State of Idaho for one of her clients. She was good at this job - she even excelled at it. But she wasn't doing what she was meant to do. And I told her so a few weeks after I met her. Our initial interactions were typical surface professional conversations but I sensed something much deeper in Courtney. It was a shared car ride from a workshop in Coeur d'Alene, Idaho to a workshop in Lewiston, Idaho that our friendship took root. From that time until today, a rich and real relationship began to flourish - one with a lot of "mirror-holding-up" and professional authenticity.

Courtney has changed. Or maybe she's just more herself than she used to be. If I had to put a label on Courtney now, it would be something like "Creative Entrepreneur". But she's still changing. She's using her broad range of knowledge and insight and reaching many corners of modern business. She understands the deep necessity for creativity in any ven- ture. She is whip smart about contemporary business practices. She has the unique ability to see the whole being of every person she meets and deftly manages conversations with top level executives as well as the barista behind the counter. In her eyes they are equal in their wholeness and their creativity.

In short, Courtney is perfectly positioned to spread the word of creativity. Her first book, *I Heart Creativity*, does just that. It introduces you to your creative self in a way that helps you make sense of the massive changes happening in society. It shows you where your forms of expression and outpourings of art add color to the world.

Why should this matter to you? Because you are part of a new creative reformation. A blending of ancient and contemporary. Your thoughts, your ideas, your influence. And most of all, *your* creativity. In this new age of the human, everyone is an artist and everyone is a consumer of art and, as Courtney will explain, *everyone is creative.*

The past few years have made it possible for anyone to make a living on their creativity. Anyone! This has never happened in the history of the world. Earlier artists relied on patrons. Then the industrial age happened and art, creativity and expression were relegated to side gigs and pursuits for those unfit for manual labor. If you are Gen X'er or older, imagine telling your parents that you wanted to be a full-time artist. As a musician, painter, poet, singer ... whatever. Unless your parents were outside of the norm, this would have been seen as folly and met with a chorus of "You'd better have a Plan B." Thanks to the digital frontier, heightened senses of community and a fresh appreciation for all things original, many, many people make a living as "professional" artists.

We have three things to thank for being the catalysts of the Age of Creativity and Humanization:

Personalized technology. It started with personalizing programming with TV remotes, then DVRs, then streaming. It moved from a group device (TV or radio) to mobile platforms where at any time you have the power to express, influence, create, share, comment, consume as you see fit. With the hypersonic additive of social media, personalized technology wrested power of brand from ad agencies and media companies and put it - literally - in the hands of you. You the consumer, voter, fan base, employee, citizen.

Art everywhere. Look around. Look at all the art! Murals on buildings, art-centric lobbies of office buildings and hotels, decor at restaurants and coffee shops, a craving for original pieces in our homes. And the enormous explosion of body art in all forms. After years and years of genericized sameness, unique is back. Different is back. Weird is hot. The Art is Everywhere movement extends beyond classic mediums to combat and counter anything that represents mass production. Rather than buy the fake apothecary table from The Pottery Barn, you scrounge through thrift shops, estate sales and Craigslist ads in search for the real thing. This further extends to taking that which has been marketed as a practical solution and infusing it with beauty. Dyson re-invented the vacuum cleaner. Not just with technology, but with design. Apple continues to blend form and function to make things we didn't know we needed. Tesla took the staid and ugly electric car market and crafted machines of beauty and performance.

Millennials. Ah Millennials. Did you just heartily cheer or sigh and roll your eyes? Well, I'm not talking about a specific age group. Although the 25-35 generation certainly has ushered in a lot of change, the Millennials I am referring to are actually ageless. They are a mindset and behavior pattern ranging from 8 to 80. The Millennial mindset has a specific set of common patterns that unite this group into what we call "Opt-In'ers". They are opting in to a new set of principles, ideas and ways of thinking. This includes the aforementioned technology adoption, but also includes a heightened sense of self-awareness and self-confidence. It includes having global relationships, exposure to a lot of different cultures. And maybe most of all, a healthy skepticism for authority and a highly sensitive BS radar.

What does this all mean for you? It means that you get to be you. Not the shape or form assigned to you by parents, teachers and other grown-ups. It means you get to return to the talents and beliefs you've had as long as you remember - yet maybe set aside for the safety of a career. This Age of the Human means that YOU are a brand. Your mission on this planet, your purpose in life, your one-in-3-billion set of skills and ideas. You are in charge. You get to decide.

I Heart Creativity is your guide on this oft terrifying journey to discover your inner creative being. With Courtney's blend of outer logic and inner wisdom, this book will ring true in your soul. It will make your heart pound - but it will pound in unison with others' awakening hearts while quieting your mind.

This book will change you. It will re-shape you. If you follow its ideas, your life will bend in new directions that were never in "The Plan."

You are ready for it.

The world awaits what you will create.

JUSTIN FOSTER
Root + River
Austin, Texas

CHAPTER 1

I HEART CREATIVITY

The creative process is fierce, and it always involves some amount of suffering, and a great deal of gratitude. Without this paradox, we cannot even hope to be truly creative, no matter who we are, where we come from, or what we do with our time and the application of creative energy.

My mission is to give you some portion of the information that I have gathered from a lot of wise people and from my personal experiences. All of it points to the fact that if we understand and embrace the universal language of innate creativity we can live much healthier, happier, balanced, more productive, fulfilling lives. And we can design new systems and bring products to market in a genuinely authentic way touching hearts and minds and producing incredible returns on investment and fundamental breakthroughs in the way we do business, match products and content, and deliver service to our customers and our community of creative colleagues.

As a collective whole and as individuals, we claim to love creativity. We love the novelty of something new, shiny, and beautiful. We love the passion and enthusiasm of a successful artist who manages to convince us that their work is special or an entrepreneur who truly breaks down a boundary and crosses successfully into uncharted territory. Creativity is quiet, delicate, warm, and safe but brash enough to evoke epic feelings of power, confidence, and wholeness.

So why are we so cruel when creativity is rolled out in a practical way? Why are we so hard on ourselves when creativity is posed as a solution instead of something expected and empirical? Why are we so reluctant to make creativity part of a regular business dialogue and place it firmly on the agenda every day when we go to work?

Simple. We're afraid of it. Creativity is the personification of quiet, and yet finding a peaceful space to pursue it can feel like an exercise in madness in the chaos of modern life. We think it must just be a blip on the radar because something so enjoyable cannot possibly take up a significant chunk of the "working" hours in our day. We think it possesses beauty but lacks value; and because we can't contain it and define it we shun it.

My creative heart has been broken hundreds of times and full to the brink of bursting at least twice as often. In spite of the ache and the damage the one abiding truth I know is this; the creative heart returns to itself, knits and heals after nearly terminal wounds, and finds a way to turn all of the holes punched in it into a constellation of stars. Light shines brighter through the damaged, creative heart, seeping through those holes and blazing supernova bright, working extra hard to illuminate the way so that the soul attached to the heart won't give up. The light shining through creates incandescence so that the next time the heart is punctured, no matter how big the knife, the wound can heal more quickly and blaze a little brighter.

Who are each of us, really? We're what's in our individual creative hearts; we're the center and the middle and the source, the essence and the soul driving the body. We're a bundle of nerve endings trying to deal with the constant of change which is served up to us every day in the modern world. We're a juxtaposition of pain, fortune, beauty, chaos, and unspeakable joy. And we're walking around in the world trying desperately to understand ourselves, to comprehend and make peace with others, and to do the work we're uniquely made and put here to do.

At our best, we're pure authenticity, but we're rarely at our best. We are the heart of darkness and at the razor's edge of destruction desperately seeking purpose and patiently waiting for the day where we can learn to love ourselves unconditionally and to truly be seen by others so that we may walk in the world in a safe, joyful, and meaningful way.

In the nexus of all of our whirling and chaos, our flying emotions and our base needs, we're inherently creative. The safest and best parts of us love to be creative and feed on it. Being creative unites us, gives us meaning and purpose, and allows us to feel like the bad in the world will at some point quiet down.

When I started my career in the pharmaceutical industry in my early twenties, I got used to the word "no". In the professional space, the high-achieving scholar in me won out over the creative soul. At the beginning, I was overseeing a corporate marketing plan for two corporate offices, and overseeing the business-to-consumer strategy for 42 very different clinical research study sites across the Continental US. I spent my days reporting to a Vice President, interfacing with and serving the needs of a demanding C-Suite who was trying to take the company public, and designing brand strategies and collateral for a high-powered Business Development team who were turning multi-million dollar deals on a monthly basis.

New thinking, sensitivity, creativity, and the connection these have to business growth was totally foreign. I had a great job which would lead to a greater career and I was advancing quickly. I still felt like there was more and it was pretty clear that this group wasn't prepared for the revolution it would take to get there.

I used to arrive in that office close to two hours before the office started to buzz. I was there with the executive assistant to the CEO and almost no one else. I could peacefully sit at my desk and get miles of work done uninterrupted before everyone arrived. I could map out visions of what the creative direction for the agencies I supervised might look like. A lot of what I mapped in that overtime ended up on the cutting room floor because it didn't match the business objectives. As soon as everyone arrived, it was all objectives against a strict business agenda, performance against a marketing plan that might or might not still be relevant, and achievement focused on taking the company public while also growing rapidly and impressing huge pharmaceutical companies with regulatory rigor and fastidious practices.

Creativity? Not so much. My soul was dying. In maybe my second month in that office, I made a promise to myself. I would leave. I would find my people. I would seek room to breathe. I would design the life I wanted and the work I wanted to do. I would help others understand what had felt like common sense since I was a kid, and I would help them develop as creative leaders.

Sometimes our souls speak. And we must listen. We feed on creativity but it doesn't filter into an organization without structure.

Here's one thing I can promise; practice makes perfect. By the time you finish this book, you'll have some ideas about what to do next. You'll feel a little bit less isolated. You'll understand that we're all our own sort of creative master.

Creativity and the practice of it are complex and never-ending. And the art of becoming a creative leader is that much more complicated but also incrementally more rewarding. You'll start to understand how the layers of creativity working in a symphony of momentum can move an organization from complacent to the lasting head of the pack. You'll understand the risks that lack of focus on creativity and its value, failure to practice creative modeling, and the esoteric lack of emotional and creative support from upper level management can spell brand disaster for even the most stable modern brand. Consistency, subtle shifts, and the simple truth of getting out of our own way will let individual people monumentally shift a tide and a paradigm.

Open your heart. Open your mind. Prepare yourself for a fuller, richer life.

Let's begin.

QUESTIONS FOR YOU:

1. What challenges with creativity are you facing at work, personally, or both? How can you turn this into a creative disruption and make change sustainable?
2. How can you fundamentally recognize and adapt to accommodate a new plan for your own creativity? What parts of the personal

creative leadership strategy make sense to you and what parts will require some support?

3. How can you fundamentally shift the creativity of your daily work, regardless of the amount of control you have within your company currently?

4. Are you happy in your current position? Is your manager responsive to this concept? How can you adapt just by changing your personal process? How can you infuse creativity into your team experience? How can you contribute to psychological safety on your team and at work?

5. If you are able to accomplish one or more of the elements above, how will this shift your company's fundamental approach for the consumer and the marketplace?

CHAPTER 2

HOW DID WE GET HERE?

For me, the rigor and the exodus from the corporate machine and my rebirth into the space of creativity was gradual, progressive, very messy, scary, and expensive. I bounced from a safe corporate job with a nice salary and growth and stability in the industry to work as the first salesperson for an emerging boutique and family wine distributor in Seattle. Though my days were filled with fun and passion and fascinating people, they were also filled with stress and debt and exposure to a business machine that put the producer and the product on a pedestal and let the business strategy slide down the slippery slope of debt and organizational destruction. I had swung the pendulum too far in the opposite direction. Flush with creativity but missing stability and structure. In this space, I started to find a creative voice, and I started to see the inherent problems in the business as it related to knitting creativity together with vulnerability and structure. I had some sense of what things could look like but wasn't yet sure how to merge wild dreams, grounded expectations, and performance results.

On my journey, when I was starting to wake up, I saw that was in the center of nearly every modern dilemma was a creative heart. When I started to define the structure of that creative heart, I started to see the highways of progress instead of the dusty road to defeat, and I began to expedite the changes I needed by using creativity as an engine for innovation, as momentum and measure for what comes next, and as both a metaphorical and an empirical measuring stick for bona fide progress.

When people have an affair with creativity but don't take it seriously and integrate it into their lives - or worse when leaders refuse to see its value and integrate it into their business - the relationship with creativity has an inevitable dark side. It's like the tempting devil on the shoulder instead of an angel creating novel combinations, enhanced productivity, and healthier, happier, more balanced employees. It's more destructive than productive, resulting in a vicious cycle that makes us debate the value of the natural state of creativity. If they feel they are entirely responsible for their own professional development but creativity is not clearly a business agenda item set by top leaders and emphasized at all layers of leadership, employees feel pressured and they shut down emotionally and put nose to grindstone, effort to task only. This murders creativity and creative flow.

According to a Pew Research study from 2016, 54% of the workforce believe that they need constant training and upgrades to their professional skills to maintain their position at work. In the same study, 72% say that they believe the responsibility of personal development falls largely on the individual, whereas in the past we might have felt that it was an organization's responsibility to choose a path of accelerated development for us and to put us on it. In 83% of those surveyed, the most important skills were social and interpersonal. That's a lot of pressure.

While we are doing all of those things are we taking care of ourselves as individuals? Are we remembering that we are catalyst and action as related to this colossal change and a creative approach to it? The constant? Change. The reality? We're moving too fast to be truly prepared for what's around the bend. Where we once valued extraordinary depth of technical skill in our leaders or managers, now we need people with creative heart who can get everyone in a state of dynamic conversation and balance and pull the talent out of the technical experts. We need captains and guides.

I am fortunate because I know—and have always known—with crystal clarity who I am and what my creative heart looks like. I didn't always know what to call it, and I didn't know the steps to take to grow it, but I can always find the center of it and trust it. And without leaning on my creativity, I wouldn't have been brave enough to love deeply and without regret, to become a wife and a mother, or to believe that I could put my voice and vision on the line and turn it into a profitable business. It's not been an easy road and the rewards have often been very difficult to see.

Today's worker wants the clarity to be creative but is afraid to seek it. They are protecting themselves from being hurt in the workplace by being too vulnerable and putting their jobs in jeopardy. Without this self-awareness and group safe space they struggle to address the risky proposition of putting unusual things together in a new order or combination on company time. If the business leaders don't support creativity as a daily business agenda item, this is truly a danger. A lot of people are shedding the corporate machine in favor of something that feels more real - both as consumers and at work. Once they have developed the self-awareness and some creative autonomy, all today's worker needs is a safe environment to practice their creative autonomy within. They need a team space where their strengths are valued and time on these is enhanced, and where other members of their team are available to balance the scales and support them on things they aren't as good at.

With both of these things in place, an organization has a firm platform for creating a new communication strategy, both internal and external, and to provide consistent support and dynamic product development to a stable, and consistently loyal community of buyers. Recently there has been a wave of research that is backing it up.

The design company Adobe has a vested interest in the evolution of the creative community and the creative person at work. For years, they have done a great job of turning creative results into white papers and studies so that businesses can substantiate and understand creativity's impact on work.

In the Fall of 2016, Adobe executed a deep research study covering the U.S., U.K., France, Germany and Japan with a demographic of people aged 18 to 65 for the most complete snapshot of our values at work. They gave all of the participants a 20-minute online qualitative survey.

Here is what Adobe's 2016 "State of Create" Research found:

Creativity and productivity go together. That's a positive outcome and as someone who has been pushing this boulder up a hill for two decades in business, it's very statistically reassuring. And it makes sense. Creativity is the engine and the momentum of innovation; it's the fuel for ideation and the fire and passion driving an organization. When it's practiced and focused it produces more business results.

Creativity pays and is measurably good for the bottom line. That's what companies have been wishing for for decades; ways to show that what is fun is also beneficial to business and will help them grow. According to the survey results, creativity seems to make people better leaders (70%), better workers (70%), parents (69%), and students (69%).

Creatives are a step ahead. Based on standard household income, creatives are earning 13% more on average, and often much more than that. Why? Their ideas and work are novel and can't be outsourced to another cog or a low-paid international affiliate. Creatives report better emotional balance, being happy, fulfilled, and energized at work.

Creativity is valuable to society and the economy. And by this, I mean the global economy. Globally, responding parties and management reported that creatively-stimulated employees are more productive (78%), have more satisfied core customers (80%), foster and move innovation ahead (83%), and are more financially successful than their peers (73%).

Of those assessed, 77% said that they feel more pressure in the modern business world to be more productive at work, but 56% said that there is an increasing pressure to be creative at work. A large percentage of the respondents worldwide (74%) said that it's important for companies to have express creativity and design in their business for maximum marketplace attraction and results.

We've finally reached a moment in time where we are measuring and validating the creative process at work. But we are putting responsibility for personal development and expanded creative capacity on employees at work.

A significant group of people are taking that cue and developing businesses of their own. And globally, we claim to love creativity.

What's the problem?

Our battle with creativity is a very personal daily and hourly battle within ourselves. Our love for it is our self-love and our disdain for it is our insecurity. For most of us, our lives have been spent learning to push creativity aside or down, to tear our handmade pictures off the wall, and, as we enter the smelly, awkward transition of puberty, to hide our creative souls from our peers for fear of being judged and deemed unacceptable. For decades, we have removed the creative process from schools, taking away art classes and intellectual query, which requires investigation and handling and novel thinking to dissect, in favor of canned test scores and the "standard" collegiate path.

And now, all of a sudden, we're meant to pivot and shift. As a matter of fact, we don't really have a choice now because what was a threat and a whisper is now a roar. Current global political dynamics—Brexit, the controversial US Presidential election of 2017, and the question of more European countries leaving the EU to name just a few—underscores a destabilization that will kill a dinosaur business in a matter of 12-24 months.

So, what do we do about this problem? How can we measure and seize the measure of a creative heart and turn what happens on a very personal internal level into a movement that can change and unite five generations of thinkers and workers under one common banner and mission? This sounds like a mission…… for the heart.

QUESTIONS FOR YOU:

1. Are you more in the creative zone or living on the shadow side of creativity?
2. Do you feel that you have a love/hate relationship with creativity personally? How does the organization you work for approach creativity?

3. Do you feel you have clarity as it relates to the ways that creativity can be beneficial and how it can shift a company?

4. If the organization you work for won't "buy the hype" and shift from old thinking to creativity, would you be happier reconsidering your professional future?

5. How do you think creativity can help unite five generations working together now and how can we grow and evolve better business practices by using creativity?

CHAPTER 3

THE GENIUS OF THE CREATIVE HEART

At a fundamental turning point in my life, I was living in Edinburgh. I had been on the brink of disappearing into my sadness and my creativity was getting cloudy. I was losing myself and I was scared. The light was moody, the sky foggy almost every morning. It rained most of the time but often it was a fine mist clinging to my wool scarf and hat and it felt like I was carrying my tears on my shoulders and the crown of my head every day. I returned home each evening with flushed cheeks, deep breaths, and a visceral desire for a cup of hot tea. I could feel the history and the heartbeat of the city — I was home.

At least once a week, I made my way up the hillside leading to Edinburgh Castle and the Royal Mile. I would stop at the top near Edinburgh University at the shops that surrounded the University library and was the gathering place for the university population. I would often end up at the art store; inhaling the smell of cold-pressed watercolor paper, spending long periods of time looking at all of the different colors of paint, running the soft brushes over my forearm, and feeling the weight of the best brush in my hand. Calm and creativity also come in the form of scent and taste, and for this my favorite reprieve was a coffee shop called The Elephant House. Inside it was cozy, intimate, and it smelled like the Pacific Northwest. A heady combination of the caramelized sugar on fresh pastries and the smoky burn and hum of the espresso machine and the whoosh, swirl, and froth of steaming milk. It was always full but never crowded and the same cast of characters were always there. I never spoke to them —just smiled at and nodded—as if we were sharing some kind of sacred common ground and a little secret. I would buy my coffee and settle in with a book or my sketch pad and some dry paints and a brush and tuck in for awhile. I could get lost in that time. Often no matter what day I would show up or at what time, the same people were there doing the same thing as I was in parallel, working on something private and intense.

There was one woman in particular who was always in one of the back alcoves, head down and working away. Sometimes a young girl was with her, and sometimes she was alone. Always, she was lost in the creative flow.

I always noticed when she was there. She didn't look up much, but she hummed with intensity. She was clearly lost in the process. I was captivated by her energy and her conviction. I wondered what she was working on.

Later, I found out that she was J.K. Rowling, head down and pushing full steam on *Harry Potter and the Sorcerer's Stone*. She had recently divorced and was left as a single parent to a young daughter. She had been rejected by 12 publishers when presenting the *Harry Potter* manuscript. Finally, in 1997, Bloomsbury decided to take a chance on her and publish the book after initial chapters had been given to the chairman's eight-year-old daughter. The Bloomsbury team gave her the advice that she would be wise to "get a day job" while she quietly tried to pursue the publication of the book because the odds of her making any money at her passion and in the creative pursuit of novels for children was "unlikely". She didn't listen. By June 1997, a limited run of 1,000 copies were printed with 500 copies given to libraries. In 1998, Rowling won the British Book Award and Children's Book of the Year. In 2001 the first Harry Potter book was published by Scholastic in the U.S., and today the total *Harry Potter* empire (books, movies, merchandise, and theme parks) is in the realm of $15 billion dollars in sales and rising.

J.K. Rowling's story is unique. She was, and is, very different. Serendipitously, she hit the mother-load. She worked against all odds though she was living on public assistance and a grant from the Scottish Arts Council, trying to bring to life something that had been gripping her heart and soul for more than a decade. She survived difficult circumstances and retained her belief in her ability to be, feel, and see more from the life she wanted, to immerse herself in the creative process. But she was relentless in her pursuit of what she knew was the right creative path, she was single focused and maintained the belief that she not only could, but would, succeed with her story of a young boy who felt stunted and stifled and unable to embrace his personal magic. The Harry Potter series and J.K. Rowling's personal story both outline the idea of unblocking creative prohibition, reaching into your soul, and living from a place of truth, grace, and complete individuality. It's even more apparent in today's business world and economy, but she knew what the rest of the world is discovering - devotion to one's unique purpose, vision and creativity are what illuminate novel combinations in stories, products, goods, and supersedes economic struggle and elevates the creative person above the average worker with a skill set that cannot be challenged or outsourced. It begins with the merging of creativity and motivation.

According to author Daniel Pink, J.K. Rowling's story follows a well-researched thread related to the genius of the creative mind and the science of motivation. His most boiled down statement from his 2009 book, *Drive*, is this: "There is a mismatch between what science knows and what business does." He elaborates later by saying, "Our current business practices are outdated, unexamined, and rooted in folklore."

According to Pink, in order to be moved to success in a creative fashion, we need three simple elements:

AUTONOMY - the urge to direct our own lives.

MASTERY - the desire to get better and better.

PURPOSE - the opportunity to be part of something greater than ourselves.

After analyzing studies from the Federal Reserve in 2005, a follow-up study conducted by the London School of Economics in 2009, and study subjects from the U.S., the U.K., and India, the results were consistent: extrinsic rewards are successful with rote tasks with simple problems and a clear destination, but creative problems with uncertain solutions that required participants to overcome unexpected hurdles and develop surprising solutions suffered if there was any expectation of compensation or reward for accomplishing the task.

We need to be moved by our own creativity. We need to be motivated by heart, our expansive minds, and our desire to be more whole, complete and satisfied, and not by the opportunity to rise on a ladder of success or to be promised a big paycheck. We crave independence, the opportunity to be the master of our own creations, and the cosmic sense that our end goal is much bigger than ourselves.

The artist and corporate business strategist Erik Wahl put it well saying, "The real difference between you and the creative leaders who inspire you is action." J.K. Rowling? Action. Average person? Inertia. What factor divides these two perspectives is genuine, soul-filling creativity and the belief in the genius of the creative heart. Why don't more people possess this? Fear. Pain. More fear. More pain. Fear, fear, FEAR. Most of us are paralyzed by the things we think we can't do and stuck in the fits and starts of creative prohibition because we don't know where to begin, what process to follow, and how to follow it to an end point with a result. What we keep forgetting is that the hobbling, winding, crazy journey is the entire point and produces creativity. And practice produces resilience for the mistakes we make along the way. And often, we strike gold with what we find on the road.

J.K. Rowling demonstrated what both Pink and Wahl have defined in great volume and during a time of enormous pressure in her personal life. She stayed the course and maintained her convictions in spite of repeated rejection because even if she didn't succeed commercially and in business the birth of her idea and the exercise of her creative practice was essential and pivotal to her emotional health and happiness. In maybe the most extraordinary way, she made an enormous amount of space to do the work, to practice her craft, and to design a whole new concept and imagined reality. She let herself fall into an ecstatic state of flow and she let it carry her through the process. She naturally followed a fundamental series of cues that lead her not only to creative liberation but to seeing the actualization of her creative heart in a commercially successful venture.

Recently, I attended a technology, web, and marketing conference called Collision. I was impressed by the level of attention this meeting of the minds gave to positive interruption, beneficial change management, and creativity. At that conference, I saw Alicia Hatch (now Chief Marketing Officer at Deloitte Digital) speak and with her perspective and conviction I saw that the concept of creative heart non-linear thinking was truly resonating at the highest levels of business, and that those who are willing to pursue a novel path from A-Z are truly changing the communications game and the face of leadership one day at a time. She told the story of a little game called Halo and how it came to market and fundamentally changed the nature of gaming, gaming consoles, and the vertical integration of go-to-market strategy. She lead that team. Halo started as a military science first person shooter game developed by a company called Bungie in the Seattle, Washington area. Extremely strong sales of the game lead to development of new games in the series, but Alicia and her marketing team were also wickedly smart. They started looking for interesting connections and found that there was a deep market for all of the other media that continued the game's story - like graphic novels and a bevy of other licensed products. When the game was acquired by 343 Industries (a subsidiary of Microsoft), the way the game was played started to affect the development of the X-Box console, which affected the development of competing consoles. Alicia and her team looked for novel combinations where they hadn't previously existed and as a result they bent boundaries and "unlocked" creativity. The Halo marketing team wasn't interested in selling one game at a time, they were creating an empire of fiercely loyal community members who wanted hands on anything connected to Halo because they were a part of it and it was the fabric of their experience.Because of their willingness to move and take risks and with a great deal of support from senior leadership, this marketing team moved around the company from department to department, developing new threads for the product wherever it made the most sense and collaborating with that department.

Did this story follow typical corporate rigor and organizational structure? No. Did it follow a common go-to-market thread or strategy organizationally? Not even a little bit. Did it require a great deal of investment of faith from top leadership and from the marketing team putting themselves on the line every day? Yes. Did it succeed? Hell, YES.

They embraced "the loyalists" and developed a commitment that only grew. Halo's use of vertical development of products and eventual connection with product placement came at a pivotal time in the marketplace as Netflix and Hulu and Amazon were rising and evolving, and fundamentally escalated the success of what would have otherwise been just another video game. And the results were measureable and patent. The Halo franchise has now netted $5 billion dollars because the people in charge of communicating around it saw a moment of transformation and serendipity, had the support of leadership, and took a risk. Once they saw the success of the risk, they didn't let it get stale - they kept adventuring and looking for new ways to connect this product to the lives of the people who purchased it and to escalate the conversation around it.

Marketing is a rogue and cowboy business in the modern world — it's unsafe, unsteady, and fraught with risk and significant reward. Creativity is a lifeline for executives who are putting their heart, soul, and careers on the line every day, fighting the tide of over-communication, dancing within a transparent marketplace, and seeking to find the million (or billion) dollar answers that will resonate with a young audience desperately seeking meaning, relevance, attraction, and connection.

Staleness and complacency have no place in the space of true creativity. It is a moment to moment exercise in new thinking. And acting with creativity and leading creatively are two different things - one must carve out and identify their own creative practice before they start to try to lead others creatively. If you admire these examples but aren't naturally wired to push from creativity into leadership, that's okay. It's a practice, like yoga or meditation.

Here are five things you can practice right away to turn a creative heart into creative leadership:

1. **Shake the tree**. Start with creative heart and instigate change even when others don't. Change is a constant. If you are concerned with rattling someone else's cage, start with your own. Model what you're looking for and look at disruption as a choice and as something that you are in control of.

2. **Listen to your creative heart.** Whoever said "hearts and minds" had the right idea but was mistaken that they could happen at the same time. Put heart and gut first and follow it up with a system. But don't go to the mind until you know the heart. Having only heart is like the stereotype of a starving artist; all passion and no product. Having only logic is a system without application of creative talent. Having both heart and mind, with the heart coming first and the system following? Epiphany.

3. **Move.** Realize that perfect is impossible. If you aren't a fast-moving personality, move fast for you. Just be willing to launch before it's perfect. Too much planning means missing the boat. Either someone else will do it sooner, or you'll overwhelm yourself with perfection of the details and it will never see the light. The beauty is in the flaws and who magnifies those and gives you new insight. Let the experimental process happen and feel free to throw out ideas that don't work. Mistakes are part of the process and force you to refine the concept.

4. **Put your foot down and set boundaries.** Have natural conviction; this is rare and only found in some leaders. Set a focused course of action with specific parameters around what you will do and what you won't do and stick to your convictions. Master your specific area of creative leadership.

5. **Imagine the future and work back to reality.** Maintain an extensive capacity for originality and practice going beyond the boundaries daily. Don't go above and beyond, go beyond the beyond. Imagine your work in a utopic state and work backwards from the future to it. Don't do the assignment, do more. Design new frontiers.

By identifying who we uniquely are as creative beings, how we are born, how we grow up, and what defines us as adults, and then by capturing our creative heart in a process, more of us can unblock our learned prohibition, re-define our creativity, and see a magnificent wave of energy carrying us to a new future.

QUESTIONS FOR YOU:

1. Are you working at your creative process? Do you acknowledge its presence and do you have a practice? What is the earliest pattern of creativity you can remember yourself engaging in?
2. Have you ever sat down and imagined what your ideal future would look like and then thought about where you are now and considered that if you built a few bridges and expanded your creative capacity, that future may not be so far out of reach?
3. Do you truly believe in the magic of your own creativity? How do you feel about the idea that you might be better at something than literally anyone else in the whole world?
4. Do you feel that you have possession of your own autonomy, mastery and purpose? What makes you autonomous? What are you masterful at doing? What makes you feel like you are helping build something bigger than yourself?
5. Are you ready to stop being precious? Are you prepared to and willing to fail?

CHAPTER 4

THE UNIQUE YOU

I live life in color. Literally. My daily experience is vastly different from the average person, and in a pretty uncomfortable way most of the time. I have a very sensitive sense of taste and sense of sound. My scent sense merges with color most of the time, so I smell in synesthesia. I am also an empath and an HSP (highly sensitive person) and can easily take on the pain and struggle of other people. All of these components make for great fuel for an artist's mind, but when I was working in a conservative corporate environment where none of this gets unleashed I felt untethered and disconnected. With these things and because of the support I received from my parents to be a creative person, I grew up in a state of constant drive to create, draw, paint, and make. I am also a very structured person who likes putting things in order and executing creative ideas as process and business plans. These things don't always match up.

The modern person at work has a magnified need to be seen and appreciated and loved for who they are, and for the humanity in them to be a part of their daily experience. It's not easy being exactly what they are. They want to weave together their work and passions and lead with their hearts. The collective attention span is short and getting shorter with each new technological efficiency. We all lack practice at making room to live, to breathe, to create something, and to revel in the process of learning how to do it as we go. In the U.S. we too often fail to mentor our younger generations with any sort of tradition, process, or ritual as it relates to connecting heart and feeling with invention and design.

We hold ourselves together with scotch tape and bated breath, with whispers of magic and lungs full of hope, and we pray it will be okay. And a lot of the time, it is. Sometimes, it most definitely is not. And when it isn't, we cannot move through the pain, suffering, and fundamental change and wish it into a pyramid of creative balance unless we tap an old reserve, a creative energy source. And to tap it, we must have previously created it, designed the space, nurtured it, filled the reserve, and refilled it along the way so that a library of resilience and a reservoir of emotional economy are available to us in our hour of need. We must have a reminder of the best of what we are, the worst of where we have been, and the magnificence of what we can become.

As children we are born like this. Creative. Resilient. Willing and able to weather change. It's innate and our belief and faith in its safety and security are whole. But the second the clock turns and shame and fear start to take the place of creative safety, the lovely, perfect little humans start tearing their creative work apart and never re-creating it, shying away from critique in favor of advancing their social capital, and beginning the death roll of creative disconnection and prohibition. In the space of modern culture where our attention spans are shot and the collective tendency is to throw a device at any child who is bored or reacts poorly, we're not helping that paradigm improve.

Creative minds are good at making mistakes. They take a risk, screw something up, ball it up, throw it at the wall and begin again. They revel in the chaos of a mountain of paper balls and the zone of striving to create something that emulates what they find in their hearts and minds. Somewhere as we age (and I think it is different for each person) our families, our peers, and our own psyche shape our willingness to be creative and exposed and our need to retract. And then as adults, after years and maybe decades of prohibition, we're asked to step into the creative dance at a high personal price and to be safe and comfortable there. Those who have the reserve and the will to use it fare better. The saddest truth is that we all have the capacity to build the reserve and the practice, but it's socially pressed out of us.

We begin whole, complete, and very creative, but the creativity is worked out of us over time. In some families creativity is nurtured and in others it is rejected, so the trajectory for creative prohibition is very different depending on how we are nurtured. It used to be that we got some measure of creativity within the school system, but now, unless kids are in a charter or a private program, often art and the pursuit of routine creativity are completely elective unless it's a common value they share with their parents, their families recognize their interest or talent, or it's worth for them in the long run.

My good friend Jessica Rolph and I met when we were both starting families. She is an extraordinary human, and I am honored to have spent part of that chapter of my life with her. She was COO/and Founding Partner of Happy Family Brands and the Happy Baby line of food and products until the company grew and was sold. Jessica has done extensive research on the ways that infants and small children are creative and learn. This is a fundamental element of the educational foundation of her professional perspective and her product line and is a part of everything that she designs and develops for children.

Jessica is uniquely amazing at what she creates and the way she thinks about and manages a business. When we met, she was in the early throes of setting up the Happy Family Brand - at the tipping point between the company really taking off and it never matching the vision she and her business partner had in mind. Over the years, I have watched her evolve an extraordinary organization while becoming a wonderful mother, and raising three small children with her husband. In 2013, when her company had tripled revenue in the space of two years, Happy Family was sold to Group Danone based in Paris. Jessica is now hard at work creating another company that benefits children and families. She's a force, a brilliant business person, and she's uniquely creative.

When I asked her about creativity in her business, she said for her it is twofold: one part in the way she approaches her business for the consumers (parents and children), and the other part in the way she manages her staff and encourages creativity in her organization. Woven into her customer approach, her process and approach are defined by the paradigm of convergent psychology vs. divergent psychology and the advantages of being challenged and forced to innovate a process.

To explain the psychology behind it a little bit, the convergent approach offers a "correct" answer to solve a problem or task and there is also an "incorrect" way, and a reward or positive feedback is given for the correct answer. We see this when we give a child the tasks that have clear and defined answers and reinforcing "correctness" while punishing "incorrectness". Think of a child's toy focused on matching shapes and forms - when the child fits a shape into a space and something lights up or offers a positive response, the child gets positive reinforcement. This is convergent psychology.

Conversely, in the divergent psychological approach, the entire task is devoted to problem solving, innovation, and creativity. Jessica explained that researchers whose work she uses in her business have found at the 10-minute mark following a feeling of boredom, children tend to push through and problem solve. Think giving a child a subject for a game and asking them to make up the rules, the process, and the interpersonal dynamics. Exercising this capability as a "muscle" goes against the norm of an over-stimulated and screen-focused society and even causes some social anxiety for parents of children who are complaining in the state of boredom, but it creates a state of making, developing, and defining that a child with convergent thinking is missing.

She explained that the same research shows that babies are hungry for divergent learning shows that we (as the adults in their lives) must avoid interrupting them and let their fascination naturally peter out in order to nurture individuals with creativity that lasts and advances. They found that children want to problem-solve and discover because their brains are rapidly developing rich, new neural networks which connect their capacity of thinking to applied innovation. When we deprive them of this opportunity to be creative - accidentally or intentionally - it results in low engagement and their neural networks start to form around things that aren't relevant to problem solving in real life.

We also discussed the way that this same concept pertains to Jessica's supervision of a major brand with an intense and specific daily vision in the role of COO. She reflected that this convergent versus divergent concept is vivid in corporate culture and she felt that it showed up specifically in teams and staff who felt like they have to have the "right" answer to please the C-Suite and grow the business. She explained that she feels modern businesses more often have due diligence than empowered teams and that she has sometimes caught herself on a quest for answers which may have made her team wonder if there was room for mistakes and learning.

Jessica is progressive and thoughtful, so her approach upon understanding this disconnect in the workplace was to revise the company's launch process for a new product, to create space for a review and conversation, and to lean into what could have been done better from the top down. Accepting responsibility for herself first, Jessica communicated to her team that efficiencies and evolution are a constant and that creativity is a core value for her company. She saw that when she supported creativity actively and consistently her team was buoyant, enthusiastic, and much more resilient when other delays and issues came up in the process. She saw that they were as hungry as her research said young children are for learning from concepts, that engagement increased, and a safety net of trust was built within the team from the top down.

So how do we deal with this phenomenon when we are communicating with fully-formed adults who have already learned to prohibit themselves? How does it go over when we receive a build-up of creative feedback that doesn't support the direction we have been heading in? Might we veer to the convergent thinking side and believe that we have done something wrong, broken a paradigm, or forgotten the rules? Creative prohibition is commonly found in the workplace and in our population of adults in the U.S. work space in general. Though I haven't found any particular studies that address the total volume of the phenomenon, I see it nearly every time I walk into a new company for a discussion. It's easy to spot; it's the smell of fear on a new or established leader when things are about to fundamentally change in the business because they are petrified that they cannot actualize the change in a positive way and they have no idea where to begin. This fear is relatable, and some of the best creative minds of our time have slowed or stopped themselves before they really hit their stride.

I met Paul Jarvis through a mutual friend and he instantly became someone I loved to communicate with. He's witty, interesting, and wickedly smart. Best of all, he is purely himself, without reservation and without apology. I started a conversation with him and soon found myself compelled to purchase his books, participate in some of his online classes, and to subscribe to his podcast. His creativity is infectious and his passion for what he does is inspirational.

Paul Jarvis is the hardest working creative you're likely to meet, and he's a renaissance revolutionary as well. In addition to being a prolific graphic designer and web developer, he's merged creativity and communication in the worlds of online learning, e-commerce, and writing. He's a fierce vegan and a pirate and hosts a hilarious and entertaining podcast with Jason Zook called "Invisible Office Hours". Paul will tell you that he has "felt creative" all his life and that he hit his biggest creative block when he realized he didn't like promoting his work and that this was a necessary evil for growing as an e-commerce-based entrepreneur. When he realized that his vision of creativity was about "not giving a fuck about what others think and just being focused on what and who you are", he found that promotion wasn't about selling, it was just about being who he was in front of the right audience and doing it with regularity and conviction.

"There wasn't one specific 'blammo' moment, but I think I started to see, over time, that people were buying my products and services more because of who I was than anything else," said Jarvis. "If people were really just buying part of me, I'd rather them have and see the real me. It's scary to be yourself and share your opinions, for sure, but I don't see things working any other way now. Plus, if someone's going to hate who you are or what you do, it might as well be who you *really* are."

Paul believes our world is getting noisy and that the most difficult task we have today is to break through the noise with pure creativity and authenticity. He also believes this requires more vulnerability and that this is a move in the right direction, no matter how uncomfortable it makes us.

These days, Paul is consistent in doing what he loves, setting boundaries for what he doesn't want to do, communicating with people on his own terms, and serving his audience. He's also been featured in *Fast Company*, *Forbes*, *Newsweek*, Buzzfeed, and more and has done work for major corporations and cultural icons but he's settled into his life's work and he's happy there. Paul is a fully actualized creative mind and a genuine artist who is learning every day. He is leagues ahead of larger businesses and well-known leaders because of his willingness to love creativity and to embrace it every day on his own terms.

I encountered Jason Zook as a positive byproduct of my connection with Paul. Jason is another creative revolutionary who works with Paul on the video and audio podcast series, "Invisible Office Hours" and collaborates with him on other professional projects. Jason's story is fascinating and even a little bit more dramatic. As I connected with Jason via email and shared some of my stories, he showed up ego-free and made himself available to answer questions about his creative process.

Jason's creative actualization came after he had built a $1M brand as Jason Sadler with IWearYourShirt and was sitting on the stage at a small conference in Fargo, North Dakota called Misfit Con, telling his story. In a moment of clarity and with the weight of the world on his heart and mind he admitted that things "weren't ok". He felt severely out of sync with his work and his business and quite simply - he wasn't happy. He set off on a quest to resolve that feeling for himself and for others. He started a new project called the Action Army, changed his name, deleted his massive audience, and reinvented his work product, his perspective, and his network entirely around his personal guiding principles and on a platform of being honest, real, and intensely vulnerable.

Jason said: "I would say my creativity was stifled in my college years. Everything was so much less about exploration and so much more about just getting whatever task/project/assignment done to get the grade I needed to move on; it was such a horrible way to foster and grow creative muscles. Once I graduated college and got out of that institution, I started to feel the freedom to create and just do stuff that was interesting to me. I would say it took a good five years to whittle away all of the college funk that still weighed on me."

Now Jason's daily work encourages people to be the best version of themselves with total honesty. He offers tools and systems that might help. He's incredibly approachable as a real human being. He takes time away from his audience to restore and regenerate creatively and comes back with answers and responsiveness.

He believes in the power of transparency.

"I believe we're going to move into a transparent economy. One where people don't care if their laptop cameras are always on. One where people don't care if their phone calls are being recorded. I believe in freedom and privacy, but I also believe the world would be an immensely better place if people couldn't hide and have lots of secrets. People tend to scoff at this idea, but I'd be up for a society where everyone knows everything and has nothing to hide."

Jason is sharing lessons he has learned but his approach isn't aggressive or intrusive and you will want to read what he says. He's a real person with a real story, he's been a huge internet success, and decided to completely dump his success and even change his name right in the height of that success to be who he really was. He was willing to throw all of that away in the name of happiness. Jason is a true creative and an artist. A self-described "unicorn", he doesn't do anything by someone else's playbook.

As I have opened myself up to true creativity, as I have released the chains of expectation and prohibition, I have found that creativity comes back to me. It's a circle and a magnet. It's no mistake that I know Jessica, Paul and Jason. It's people like this who have found creative center and live from the truest place who are able to bring creativity to a different place in the world, and light the way for those who are still struggling to find the bravery to emerge, recognize their talents, and open the creative door for someone new.

QUESTIONS FOR YOU:

1. Who are you really when no one is watching? What do you need and want from your life and from your work creatively? What puts you in a state of happiness and balance?
2. What makes you feel like you are in charge of your own destiny? What defines a sense of creative independence for you and a sense of purpose in your work, even if you are someone who prefers to work on a team or for a very structured company? Where is your voice in all of that?
3. What stirs your interest and longing on a daily basis? What part of your work gets you out of bed in the morning and, if there is nothing, what can you do to change that?
4. What sort of support do you find yourself ready and able to offer others in the workplace? What support do you get in return? How could you escalate this exchange in your daily professional experience?
5. Are you comfortable with total exposure? With the high of success and the reality of failure? Are you willing to show the dirty underbelly to your boss, your colleagues, and the world? If you aren't, what would make this easier for you?

CHAPTER 5

HOW YOU GOT LOST

In a world where everything is super-connected, there are a lot of lonely people. There is an extreme lack of grounding and connection to one's root cause, and core, and creative heart and soul. What specifically causes us to feel this lost? Why do we walk around in the world feeling un-tethered and disconnected? Even some of the most creatively present and focused people I have met have this feeling, and the only thing that separates them from the general population is their ability to acknowledge it, verbalize it, accept it, and try to actualize the required change around it. Frequently, they might even sacrifice their own comfort for the actualization of this change, and in every case their status as a creatively actualized soul is because they have reached a state of understanding about who they truly are, their precise location on the road, and which steps will put them closer to greatness.

Chris Guillebeau is an excellent example of this. Before I ever met Chris or communicated with him directly, I saw him on a massive stage. He came on stage at the opening of World Domination Summit 2015 vibrating with energy, so excited to be there, and shaking like a leaf. Chris didn't appear to be all that interested in having the spotlight focused on him, but he was so driven by his conviction to bring people together with the mission of a creative collective connectedness and positive content created there that he seemed to be willing to put his own needs aside to serve the greater good. A young man, prolific author, and world traveler— he has truly mobilized a global generation and yet he was overwhelmed.

There were thousands of people gathered to see the speakers he had organized and the themes the conference explored and to meet in every moment of down time to further this mission and movement. Later, in a fluke of circumstances, I ended up exchanging emails with Chris about some common ground in our personal experiences and found that in spite of his high profile he was very approachable and willing to communicate with one human at a time. He hadn't lost his humanity in the noise of popularity, relative celebrity, and success.

Chris wasn't lost, but he'd had stumbling blocks reconciling himself with his nature and his nature with his creative purpose. When I asked him about any big epiphany in his creative workflow process, he said this: "I'm not sure it was a genuine epiphany, but I've always been fairly sensitive and for a long time I saw it as a weakness or something to overcome; somewhere along the way I realized that it was actually a gift. There are a lot of people in my community who are also sensitive, introverted, or who otherwise feel 'outside the circle' in different parts of life. Being able to relate and welcome them is one of the things I feel most proud of."

Chris was willing to admit that he was vulnerable in a way most people don't want to acknowledge and that it opened him up as an artist, a writer, and an organizer of souls. Creativity exposes us and makes us vulnerable. Introverted, extroverted, and showing his sensitivity or not, Chris' work speaks for itself and people see who he really is at his creative core. For those who feel blocked or creatively lost, that's the mission of coming back and being found. The average person has all of these feelings and questions, but without a creative structure or a heart and a center to what they are pursuing, they don't have the roadmap and the tools to plot a course that changes their way and lets them be found. They get locked down by shame, blame, confusion, rejection, and fear and feel isolated, burned out, and alone. Chris may have been at his max dealing with a large crowd, but creativity is his center and his commitment is time.

My colleague and close personal friend, Andy Johnson, is an extraordinary human being and creative on a wide and deep scale. He's moved through a colorful professional sequence with a consistent focus on his care for people, expression of creativity, and his relentless pursuit of justice and the truth. Andy is not only an amazing person, he's also a brilliant organizational psychologist and a licensed counselor and a phenomenally-creative and sensitive person. He believes that we get lost and creativity dies when it's prohibited as a practice in childhood and we are directed to other pursuits. He believes we lose ourselves in shame.

Here is how Andy put it: "Shame-based cultures almost killed me and certainly stifled my creativity. It is very vulnerable to put yourself out there when you speak every week and try to be transparent. I'm still recovering from two periods of shame in my current role. I'm now pursuing creativity mainly in my thinking, writing, and speaking on relevant issues of organizational and individual psychological health. The degree to which the people around me are 'safe' has an effect on my ability to be truly creative. It's a work in progress and better some days than others."

We express creativity when we feel safe, open, and willing to show ourselves to the world. And the only way we can fully unlock prohibition is to explore and uncover some of the hurt from our world and try to minimize it in the future. Beginning sometime around 2004, and as recently as the close of 2016, companies like Google and Adobe have been designing, refining, and validating the research of creativity and the nature of safe psychology at work because it's timely and it's vital.

Later in my conversation with Andy he said: "If the world were safer, we could be vulnerable more readily with each other. If there were less shame and competition, we could collaborate with our best and authentic selves with each other. I would predict that if we can humanize the world again (empathy, self-awareness, vulnerability, trust, etc.) that creativity would flourish as never before. We have all the tools we need, we just need to overcome the imbalance we have had for so long toward yang. This cut-throat competitive culture is killing creativity. This is also a diversity issue. A creative leadership path is a path that is uniquely suited to each person as a leader, not a cookie cutter approach. Because we've taken the latter approach for quite some time, we haven't been incubating the best group of diverse leaders that we could have. I hope that changes in the future."

Andy has helped magnify this critical point for me; creative prohibition is not something that happens to us once or all at once and then can be fixed or cured in one fell swoop. It's a chipping away at our creative psyche that we have to push against daily and a choice we have to make in overcoming it, long after we have grown into adulthood and even after if we have stepped into careers where we have total flexibility with our personal leadership. This point is underscored by research being done inside major corporations, and the ways that they are adapting their leadership to involve creativity and humanity are magnificent.

QUESTIONS FOR YOU:

1. Can you remember a time from when you were young when you felt shame in connection with creativity? Is there a memory like this from more recently - say in your adult life and at work? What was the result of that feeling for you?
2. Do you feel that the concept of creativity at work results in inclusion or division? Do you think that creativity could help heal some of our conflicts in the workplace and our lives?
3. What do you think the connections between sensitivity and creativity look like? How might this impact a person in the workplace? Are we too quick to classify ourselves and others and isolate ourselves from the expansive thinking creativity might offer?
4. When do you remember first feeling creatively prohibited? Did it last (and is it still happening) or were you able to break down the wall and turn it into creative energy at a young age? Do you feel that wall rise periodically when you are under stress? How do you break it back down?
5. How might creativity connect us with a new level of global thinking? What could creativity do to help aid us in putting people at work in new roles that better serve the business purpose but also magnify their raw talent and behavioral nature?

CHAPTER 6

WHO HURT YOU?

Much of our prohibition comes from fear of repeating a painful experience. With the research of scientists like Marie Forgeard and Dr. Martin Seligman, we now know that trauma can either block us or break us wide open creatively and create fertile ground for a garden of new thinking, emotional resilience, and innovation. I have been hurt. I am sure you have been too. In order to move through prohibition to creativity, we must be willing to ask and answer a very difficult and personal question - who hurt you?

I have more than one tragedy under my belt walking through this life. More than two or even three. Each has been a fundamental turning point for me, breaking down the walls of my own creative prohibition in a manner that was distinct and specific and leaving me more resilient and stronger. I can mark these shifts back to the day, the hour, and nearly the minute - what was happening, who I was with, what the weather felt like, what I ate, how the plants and flowers looked, what I smelled.

In 7th grade biology, I met Adrian. He was witness to and fundamentally connected my first creative transformation, the identification of my creative voice, and the rooting of my creative soul.

He didn't hurt me - but losing him did.

We became lab partners. We laughed. Really, really hard. We shared a force field. We connected and plugged in. I felt safe, and happy, and protected. He did too. No one outside really saw or understood but we didn't need them to. We each had a network of close friends, but our friendship and clarity was different from everything else. We were powerful together. From 8th grade through senior year in high school, words were our vice, and film was our love language. We had similar struggles and similar views on the world. We helped each other. Buddy-breathing our way through adolescence everything was sort of right with the world. I held back sometimes but I admired the fact that he was intrinsically brave, naturally vulnerable, honest, raw, and rare. He was believable and available. He loved hard and had fire. He struggled, but he didn't retreat.

As we got older, the "crazy" threads we followed when we first met were replaced with real ones. We were exploding into adulthood and we had choices. We compared notes on our hearts' desires for college and adult life and work and saw the possibilities of working on it together in the long run. Contrasting talents, symmetry, support. Bigger dreams. Belief that we could. Our friendship would support it. We were going to start a war against creative prohibition and the silencing of creative voices and change things for good. I started to believe that my artist's soul could co-exist with a responsible future with the support of people like him. We could see through each other. We were trailblazers who knew what we wanted and were confident we could pull it off side by side. Every creative victory was news that was quickly shared. Ideas turned into plans.

And then - one brutal day in December - he was gone.

In the aftermath of his death - and when I let myself grasp this burning slash of time in the universe - something standing outside of me saw where I was standing, all alone for the first time in a long time, for what it was. It hurt like hell, but it made sense. I was aflame with fury and pain.

Months passed. I lost faith in my ability to take on the world and change anything because I was on my own. But creativity was seeping out of me like sap from a tree. My work with a paintbrush got vivid and heated. He was dead and I was alive. In spite of the excruciating pain I knew I could never totally shed, he was still there in the background of everything. He was the whisper of my creative soul telling me what to do and how to be safe and urging me to be happy and to be real. He was the nagging reminder that I had a much bigger reason to survive and thrive. What we had accomplished together and the influence he had on me put voice to what I needed to move and change. I had work to do. I had people to help.

Barely a year after he died, I was soaring over the North Pole to make a home in Scotland. I had been 21 years old for 16 tender days. I felt a huge turning happening in my heart and mind. The heat was evaporating and the cool air was blowing again. I was inhaling more deeply than I had in a very long time. The world was starting to be mine again. My voice was shaky but clear and strong and new. The prohibition fell away. I could reclaim my place in the creative fabric and I could advance. I could still lead. I could still change things. And I could still take him with me.

I looked out at the brilliant sunrise peeking through the thick clouds as we soared, and I picked up Adrian's bravery and his passion and put it on my shoulders with mine, and I began again. Every day was an extreme dedication to creative purpose, and striving to help other people find a way. I was hurt, but I was evolving. And I was genuinely better. And some part of me was aware that I would be hurt again, but I would repair and heal and I would be okay. I could use this voice to find people and places to anchor myself to and to color my life on my own terms.

This would steel me through the other traumas and tragedies I would face as I got older. These experiences got personal in a variety of different ways. They threatened the happiness of my family and my children. They challenged my ability to emerge from the haze of despair and tragedy and fight back. And each experience taught me a sort of warrior's fight and resilience, a desire to help others learn how to find new depths within themselves and to fight for their ability to stay on the road, to be themselves, and to never give up in the pursuit of their creative happiness. These experiences have given me the innate ability to "un-prohibit" myself rapidly and to actualize what Brene' Brown says about being in the midlife stage of things: "When the Universe grabs your shoulders and tells you "I'm not fucking around, use the gifts you were given."

In his book *David and Goliath*, Malcolm Gladwell explores two ideas: the first is that much of what we consider valuable in our world arises out of lopsided conflict because overwhelming odds produce greatness and beauty, and the second is that we consistently misperceive these kinds of conflicts because we misinterpret "the giant". We fail to see that the shadow side of strength is great weakness, and we forget that just the mere fact of being the underdog sometimes wins the day because it changes people, opens doors, and creates opportunities.

Pop-culture wise, and particularly in a traditional workspace, "creativity" is just the candy jar or the icing on the cake. But true creativity often stems from pain and suffering and our progressive and consistent creative growth comes out of this. And in most people, once unleashed, creativity is persistent and loud, and must be processed in order to be quieted and aggregated into the stream of life. I often find my mind brimming with new ideas - particularly when I'm inspired by other people's creativity - and I am required to put pen to paper until the noise quiets down enough for me to return to the regular scheme of things. I have learned to organize these thoughts so that I can return to them, makes sense of them, and give them life and purpose when I am ready and that they are complete and whole and prepared to be critical ingredients in a new plan when I am ready for them. Without this processing and physical unblocking of my creative pipeline, I find myself distracted, lost in the clouds, and unable to re-anchor myself with people and relax into what they offer me and the ideas that they express.

Our needs run deep and they stem from a very base level. If we haven't had our essential basic needs met, we don't have the luxury of moving into a creative space - but as a paradox - limiting some of these needs stimulates additional creative rumination.

Follow me here. At the top of the pyramid, when all the other needs are met, self-actualization (or if I may paraphrase, "being what you're born to be" or "actualizing your creative purpose") and the transcendence of pouring out that talent to the world for the greater good are at the uppermost echelon of human existence. I put immersive practiced creativity and creative leadership at the point of that pyramid with almost a waterfall effect to each of the layers below.

But when one of the primary base needs is not met (or when someone hurts you) you must retreat to repair and re-establish that layer and its wholeness before you graduate back up to the peaks of self-actualization and self-transcendence. That pain, tragedy, trauma, recovery, acknowledgement, and repair leads to what is called post-traumatic growth. What is post-traumatic growth? Psychologists define it as the retrospective perception of positive psychological changes that take place following traumatic events, occurring in different ways: through improved personal relationships, discovery of new possibilities in life, increased self-confidence and inner strength, heightened spirituality, or a renewed appreciation of the joy of life, with many survivors describing their lives as being stronger than ever due to the hardships they experienced. Turns out that my personal experience with trauma, tragedy, and heightened creativity is not at all unique. It's pretty common and it's well documented by researchers like Marie Forgeard and creative mainstays like Mihaly Csikszentmihalyi.

In trying to understand this, I went back to the basics of Abraham Maslow's research related to this paradigm. Here is what I found. Maslow's "Hierarchy of Needs" is a theory in psychology proposed in his 1943 paper "A Theory of Human Motivation" in *Psychological Review*. Maslow subsequently extended the idea to include his observations of humans innate curiosity. His theories parallel many other theories of human developmental psychology, some of which focus on describing the stages of growth in humans. Maslow used the terms "physiological", "safety", "belonging" and "love", "esteem", "self-actualization", and "self-transcendence" to describe the pattern that human motivations generally move through. Maslow's hierarchy of needs is often portrayed in the shape of a pyramid with the largest, most fundamental levels of needs at the bottom and the need for self-actualization and self-transcendence at the top.

The most fundamental and basic four layers of the pyramid contain what Maslow called "deficiency needs" or "d-needs": esteem, friendship and love, security, and physical needs. If these "deficiency needs" are not met—with the exception of the most fundamental (physiological) need—there may not be a physical indication, but the individual will feel anxious and tense. Maslow's theory suggests that the most basic level of needs must be met before the individual will strongly desire the secondary or higher- level needs. Maslow also coined the term "meta-motivation" to describe the motivation of people who go beyond the scope of the basic needs and strive for constant betterment.

Physiological needs are the physical requirements for human survival. If these requirements are not met, the human body cannot function properly and will ultimately fail. Physiological needs are thought to be the most important; they should be met first.

Once a person's physiological needs are relatively satisfied, their safety needs take precedence and dominate behavior. This level is more likely to be found in children as they generally have a greater need to feel safe.

Safety and Security needs include:

- Personal security
- Financial security
- Health and well-being
- Safety net against accidents/illness and their adverse impacts

After physiological and safety needs are fulfilled, the third level of human needs is interpersonal and involves feelings of love and belonging. This need is especially strong in childhood and it can override the need for safety as witnessed in children who cling to abusive parents.

Deficiencies within this level of Maslow's hierarchy can adversely affect the individual's ability to form and maintain emotionally significant relationships in general.

This can reveal gaps in:

- Friendship
- Intimacy

- Family
- (CREATIVITY?)

According to Maslow, humans need to feel a sense of belonging and acceptance among their social groups, regardless whether these groups are large or small. This need for belonging may overcome the physiological and security needs, depending on the strength of the peer pressure.

All humans have a need to feel respected; this includes the need to have self-esteem and self-respect. Esteem presents the typical human desire to be accepted and valued by others. People often engage in a profession or hobby to gain recognition. These activities give the person a sense of contribution or value. Low self-esteem or an inferiority complex may result from imbalances during this level in the hierarchy. Once people form the bonds of intimacy and trust their friends and family they can take on the opportunity to look at the world differently - to put their own stamp of approval or change on things, and to explore interesting edits to the way things are so that the world looks more like what manifests creatively in their minds. Without the base needs met, this capacity is intrinsically and principally limited.

"What a man can be, he must be." Maslow believed that to understand this level of need, the person must not only achieve the previous needs, but master them. In his later years, Maslow explored a further dimension of needs, while criticizing his own vision on self-actualization. The self only finds its actualization in giving itself to some higher goal outside oneself, in altruism and spirituality.

"Transcendence refers to the very highest and most inclusive or holistic levels of human consciousness, behaving and relating, as ends rather than means, to oneself, to significant others, to human beings in general, to other species, to nature, and to the cosmos".

In a research study published in *Psychology of Aesthetics, Creativity, and the Arts*, Marie Forgeard of the University of Pennsylvania conducted survey research looking at perceived self-creativity and how it relates to adverse life experiences. Mihaly Csikszentmihalyi has suggested that creativity may stem from the need for children at an early age to take on adult responsibilities and mature more rapidly than other children in their age group. Traumatic early experiences can also lead to greater social isolation and a tendency to ignore social conventions or rules—something seen in many intensely creative people.

While research has largely focused on famous artists, writers, and composers, post-traumatic growth can provide almost anyone with a creative inspiration that may not have existed previously. According to assumptive world theory, adverse experiences tend to shatter our assumptions about life and how the world is meant to be. As old assumptions, once taken for granted as being true, are set aside, people making sense of their experiences form new assumptions about themselves and the world through a process of rumination. Along with intrusive rumination—unwanted thoughts relating to the traumatic event—deliberate rumination also lets people explore their experiences to try to make sense of what happened.

Through the cognitive processing underlying intrusive and deliberate rumination, people who are open to new experiences can gain fresh insights and "creativity" from even the most traumatic events. With the help of professionals, it is vitally important to move from rumination, which focuses on unwanted thoughts, to processing, which is unpacking and unwinding an experience with support and on your own terms. Given that almost everyone can think of a difficult or challenging situation and that the relative definition of "trauma" or "tragedy" covers a lot of ground, I'd assert that most of the population is walking around with a virtual library of creativity bottled up in their hearts and souls. Several people experience at least one lifetime trauma or tragedy so taking this experience and breaking it down for what it is and what it offers us in the way of an opportunity is a very good thing. These same researchers believe that creativity and trauma are correlated in both directions, that trauma leads to creativity, and that those who are highly creative cope better with trauma. Cope better with the unfairness life hands us? That alone seems like an amazing reason to cultivate accelerated creativity.

Take a moment and think about your life. Map backwards to your time as a small child and remember where you began. If you have enough time and emotional distance to pursue the thinking and digging behind some of those experiences, organize the map, and track the value it may produce for you. I could generally explain my way of doing this but it is a delicate process and for many people would be best guided by a professional therapist, counselor, or psychologist so that any intrusive rumination remaining can be demolished or re-channeled appropriately.

This kind of creative processing can let us review where we have been and what we give our energy to in the future based on our aspirations and personal needs. It's a key part of the personal leadership planning process that can be intensely private and incredibly illuminating. Though we may never let these private details be seen by colleagues, managers, or even people very close to us, the awareness of the existence of these things shapes the way we help ourselves exist in a professional environment - letting us defend ourselves and support others in equal measure, without resentment or anger. When these things are woven into the fabric of a personal leadership plan before we enter a work space, they become a way to have a voice, regardless of our state of extroversion or introversion, and as a protection buffering our sensitivity from destruction in a data-driven corporate space.

With proper support it can be positive to stare the old darkness down, look it in the eye, steal the light from it, and release it – letting the space it leaves fill up with creativity. You might breathe differently. You'll look at the world with kindness and peace. You can live outside of that hurt. And inevitably you'll illuminate someone else's world with your story.

QUESTIONS FOR YOU:

1. Who hurt you? When? Where? How? What was the impact to your sense of yourself and your ability to design the life you desire?
2. How did you change and grow and stretch because of this?
3. What differentiators, passions, and expertise do you bring to your work as a result?
4. Has this experience made you more connected and empathetic to others or caused you to step back and isolate yourself more?
5. How can you become more creatively balanced at work by thinking about these things?

CHAPTER 7

FINDING YOUR CREATIVE NATURE

Creativity is an enigmatic beast because, though we love to ponder it (and maybe make friends with it) the most difficult thing to do is to accept it, recognize it in ourselves, and integrate it fully into our lives.

I am not one to use labels. However, when pointing out traits and patterns to help people to see qualities and possibilities in themselves that they wouldn't otherwise see, I am in favor of them as a framework. The reluctance in our inherent creative nature to draw these lines is often why we self-classify out of the creative paradigm and lose our creative root. To root, we must find ourselves creatively and put our individual identities firmly in the center of actualizing creativity that maximizes the experience at work; to start connecting with our own creative complexities. We can begin to realize supportive creative patterns in the people we surround ourselves with; to initiate and maintain a decriminalization of "becoming creative" and to see that it doesn't have to be daunting or emotionally taxing.

In her book about the college admissions process and the thinking that young adults and their parents engage in when plotting a course for higher education, my great friend and colleague Lisa Fisher explores the idea of "appetites".

Here are some of the questions she poses:

- What am I hungry for?
- What am I craving?
- What would be satisfying to me?
- What do I need to feel sustained?

In the space of creativity and understanding our nature, we often don't ask ourselves questions and don't try to dig to the bottom and uncover who and what we really are, what we are truly capable of, and what forces we can maximize and minimize to get there. Lisa has created a new method for the thinking process about higher education that is based on these appetites and on the concept of design. Employing her method and apply-ing it to creativity when we look at our appetites merged with design, we see that "creativity" becomes less of a description and more of an action.

Lisa's work encourages students leaving high school education in the U.S. to pursue a different level of thinking as it relates to what comes next in their lives. It's very interesting—and a little bit disturbing—to me that we, as adults, have typically never taken the time to think this way or take these steps and yet we look at our workplace and our mindset and feel that something is missing, broken, or out of sync.

It might be time to take a closer look at the pursuit of our creative appe-tites and the merging of that appetite and our nature.

When you look under the behavioral hood of human nature, you see a phenomenal complexity and some simple truths. Our nature, as it relates to the way we respond to things innately, is largely seeded by the time we are around 14 years old. Trauma, tragedy, and extreme stress can shift that dial though and it may shift back or it may be altered more perma-nently. What motivates that nature is always in flux, and though it may not change our nature, it will definitely color the reality of how we deal with the world. It may change what we feel is important, how we react to our environment and people around us, and how we deal with their responses to us.

Robert Epstein is Senior Research Psychologist at the American Institute for Behavioral Research and Technology and then former editor-in-chief of *Psychology Today* magazine. Three of his 15 books, including *The Big Book of Creativity Games*, are about creativity. He also writes for the *Harvard Business Review*. Robert created competency measures based on the psychological theory of David C. McClelland and his work in the 1970s. This work shows that performance in certain categories is not only measurable but also trainable.

We are all creative. We all have creative heart. We have to exercise the creative heart as a muscle. Certain behaviors compliment that exercise and help to contain, support, and nurture practical creativity. But not everyone is naturally cut out to be a creative leader, to lead with their actions and practice and to pull these competencies out of others effectively. That isn't a stopping point or a blockade. Creative leadership is a skill grown and developed by dropping prohibition and implementing routine, practice, discourse, and consistency. Robert Epstein's study helps us validate and measure some of the ways that this is true.

Epstein and his colleagues identified four core competencies or patterns which help individuals express more creativity and which sometimes help boost creativity dramatically. If we can recognize these patterns in ourselves and practice them, our proficiency creatively and our ability to apply that proficiency to the pursuit of creative leadership becomes manageable and tangible.

A person who is likely to be more creatively expressive will:

Broaden knowledge and skills: Deliberately acquires knowledge and skills well outside one's current areas of expertise.

Capture new ideas: Preserves novel ideas as they occur, without first judging or editing them.

Manage surroundings: Surrounds oneself with diverse and novel physical and social stimuli.

Seek challenges: Seek challenges and manages failure constructively.

Epstein published a study in 2012 which showed that of more than 13,000 people in 47 countries who showed any of the four, Capturing New Ideas (#2) has the most impact on people's creative output. A creative person could be in the habit of recording ideas or inspiration with a voice memo on their phone, completing threads in Evernote, or even curating Pinterest Boards on a commuter train.

In an earlier chapter, I posited that though everyone has the capacity to be creative, it is much more difficult and complicated to become a creative leader. Epstein's study dug deeper on this issue and identified eight competencies that help managers elicit creativity in their subordinates, suggesting that some people are better than others at practicing their own creativity and others are gifted at pulling creativity out of others, or some people might be adept at both. They conducted a recent study with an ethnically-diverse sample of 1,337 managers in 19 countries (mainly the U.S. and Canada) and were able to rank the eight managerial competencies according to how well they predicted desirable outcomes in the workplace, such as how much creativity subordinates express, as reported by their managers.

The eight creative competencies most practiced by managers were as follows:

1. **Creatively competent managers challenge subordinates.** They give people difficult problems to solve and ambitious goals to reach while also helping them to manage stress and a balanced life.
2. **Creatively competent managers encourage broadening.** They provide people with training in subject areas well outside their current areas of expertise.
3. **Creatively competent managers encourage capturing.** They create space and encourage people to preserve their new ideas and provide tools and systems that make it easy for them to capture such ideas.
4. **Creatively competent managers manage their teams appropriately.** They design diverse teams with changing memberships and use pivoting, disruption, shifting, brainstorming, and other techniques to maximize the team's creative output.

5. **Creatively competent managers model the core competencies of creative expression.** These managers show others that they, as a supervisor, practice one or more of the core competencies of creative expression regularly and with dedication.

6. **Creatively competent managers provide adequate and appropriate resources to maximize their team's creative efficiency.** They provides materials, tools, continuing education, coaching, and time needed for subordinates to solve problems or generate new products or methods.

7. **Creatively competent managers provide a dynamic and changing physical and social work environment.** They intentionally manifest a dynamic and interesting physical and social work environment and alter it periodically.

8. **Creatively competent managers provides positive feedback and recognition.** They reward people for contributing new and valuable ideas.

In analysis of the study, by far the most valuable creative competency that correlated to managerial proficiency proved to be "creatively competent managers provide adequate and appropriate resources" (#6). This recommendation mirrors the recommendations of Art Markman at the University of Texas at Austin. He contends and maintains that those managers and organizations who want their people to be more creative need to give them more free time to think.

The next most valuable competency was "creatively competent managers provide a diverse and changing environment" (#7). Change the lighting, the color, the setting (work offsite). Move desks and furniture around. Bring in seasonal plants. Give people different options; darker spaces with focused light, natural light, private or quiet space, and group gathering and ideation space. Sadly, the study very clearly reflected that most managers are generally only so-so at managing creativity. The group average score on the test was a disappointing 68%, with managers consistently scoring high in only two areas: "provides positive feedback and recognition" (#8) and "encourages broadening" (#2). Though these are the simplest and most obvious ways to encourage creativity they are not the most powerful and don't fundamentally lend to growing and developing the business.

Interestingly (and very unexpectedly) the study also suggested that women are better at managing creativity than men. The researchers expect that this is because women as a group are more supportive, more willing to listen, and more likely to give people the emotional and physical space they need to think. Women outscored men by a statistically significant margin in all eight competency areas and was an impressive consistency in the data.

Robert Epstein's analysis of the study and its outcomes was this: "Creativity, like leadership, can be broken down into measurable, trainable competencies, and providing such training pays off both with more creative output and more money. Sooner or later, we need to drop the shroud of mystery in which we have long cloaked creativity and get on with the serious business of enhancing it. Competencies are the key."

Teams can use Epstein's competency assessment to see where different team members and managers stand creatively. Assessments like these are valuable and an interesting quantification of a moment in time, but they are not worth get stymied or stopped if the score isn't high. As Epstein himself says, "it's all about practice, process, and faith"… and I might add — creative heart?

Visit this site for an analysis of creative competencies:
http://MyCreativitySkills.com

To measure creative leadership and managerial skills visit:
http://MyCreativitySkills.com/managers.

In most societies (at least in the U.S. and the Western World, for the past two decades) we have been living with and promoting a standard that says we learn everything that's important to succeed in business in our collegiate and post-graduate education, and the more prestigious the University or advanced the degree we achieve, the more naturally successful we will become in business. But the "Adobe Creates" study done in five countries in October 2016 proved that we might be missing something vital with this approach.

The major gap we see widening in global business is one of inventive and creative leadership, interpersonal connection, empathy, and nuanced soft skills. These and creativity are universally useful in moving a business from disruption to managed change, and they are also some of the only skills that are not able to be outsourced. They create novelty in terms of individual talent. Google and other companies have given us volumes of new research to prove that, in spite of previous paradigms of measurement, vulnerability, positive and safe communication, and soft skills are the only things that genuinely create stable growth and productivity on teams.

Along with their proclivity for creativity, these studies are proving that women are the best at these creative humanity skills in a more natural way. What used to be called soft skills are now the some of the most coveted skill-sets in the business world, now and for the foreseeable future. Many modern female leaders naturally spend time mastering the people process. Their business experience and inherent personality traits give them the ability to connect with and motivate people. They can easily advocate and facilitate between different groups, sectors, and departments, and run interference between technical and creative parties to launch major products.

The ability to be compassionate, empathetic, sensitive, and human, and to create a safe psychological space are a sought-after combination lead by companies like Google because their research has proven that these factors have more empirical bearing on ROI and high performing teams than any of the performance objectives that had been meticulously outlined and prescribed for hiring for decades. Google recently commissioned a three-year study called "Project Aristotle" that attempted to determine the factors of a productive team. What distinguished the good teams from the bad was the way people treated each other. High-performing teams had high social sensitivity characterized by trust, mutual respect, and real connections. As baby boomers retire for next decade at a rate of 10,000 per day, they will be replaced by young female leaders who put a premium on communication, community, relevance, and meaningful connection. Welcome to a whole new era of leadership with young female executives as the new powerhouse leaders.

At the end of each day, I try to take 15 minutes to write in a creativity journal. I record one good thing and one difficult thing that happened to me that day, one way that I grew creatively, one thing I can learn from, and one thing I can put on someone else's plate. I always write on paper and with a specific pen. When I have the time I spend about twice as much time and draw out the concepts with hand lettering, icons or drawings to demonstrate my thinking. For me, this closes the door at the end of each day and gets the day's activities out of my system, putting me in a neutral space for creativity the next day. These journals show patterns which make it easier to develop solutions for recurring conflicts. When I am diligent with this practice, I see a shift in my effectiveness and overall satisfaction.

QUESTIONS FOR YOU:

1. What are you creatively hungry for? How can you satisfy that craving?
2. What are your key creative competencies? Do you think you're naturally creative in a leadership role?
3. What is your greatest soft skill? How do you use it daily? How does it help you flex creatively?
4. What is your weakest soft skill? How does it limit you? Can you see a way to develop or refine it?
5. Are you good about capturing new ideas and seeking creative challenges?

CHAPTER 8

DEFINING CREATIVE LEADERSHIP

Creative professionals used to be a specific category of worker in the knowledge economy, confined to their own imaginative roles and asked to do whatever upper management requested—no more, no less. Today, things are a little different. In a 2014 Adobe study, 82% of companies reported a strong connection between creativity and the bottom line. Yet 61% said they didn't see their own organizations as terribly creative. If we are experiencing a creativity gap, it exists nowhere more clearly than in leadership and most glaringly in the C-Suite.

In my work, I use a combination of behavioral assessments which focuses on an empirical "reflection" that the person in question offers of their own behavior and their reactions to their environment. I also use an assessment focused on the way the world or the marketplace sees that person for a reverse view and reflections on executive presence. We work on a detailed creative competency analysis, use a sensitivity assessment, and a detailed query about balance, life, and support. From this "diagnosis" we have a detailed snapshot which we can plot and organize and draw out elements for a creative personal leadership plan and a web for all of the choices we make together putting things in order for them. We have a structure for long term futuristic thinking and even to begin to imagine their parachute strategies — what they want to do after their core business goals are actualized. These are the foundations of advanced creative leadership, and I have seen some phenomenal changes in leaders who invest hearts and minds in this process.

Truly creative leaders have the competitive edge:

Creatively actualized professionals know the right way to self-promote. Some worry that self-promotion distracts from the creative process, while others see creative and business pursuits, including the messaging around them, as complementary. But for better or worse, many creative leaders have grown up used to being their own advocates in a world of intensifying competition for attention.

Creative leaders are ideal candidates to head boardroom discussions where success hinges on reconciling opposing viewpoints. When they're young, it's simply about getting people to understand what they're doing and why. Later, creatives need to compete for recognition and to land major projects. As a result, anyone who has had to defend their work in order to build a career is likely to succeed in leadership. Why? Simply put, those experiences translate into powerful leadership skills.

Creatives have essentially been honing their communication abilities and knack for strategic self-advocacy their entire professional lives. Those skills help them explain their visions to others and communicate why others should pay attention. What's more, the reasons they're likely to give have less to do with themselves than with their work and ideas–an important condition for gaining others' support

Creatively unblocked professionals act as diplomats and interpreters. Creatives are comfortable playing the roles of envoy and translator. They have experience explaining the concepts and making connections between different ideas to a variety of people, all with their own perspectives. When they move into leadership roles, this quality helps creative thinkers push different people and departments to understand one another on more than just a tactical level.

Creatives tend to feel deeply, tapping into others' elation and tribulation. At the same time, they're sensitive to the outer world, and this compassion helps them empathize with people inside and outside their organizations in ways that more analytical leaders might not be able to do. As the workplace shifts away from traditional, hierarchical management structures, this gives creatives a wider advantage in everything from building a more open work culture to recruiting younger talent and keeping everyone motivated for the right reasons.

Creative thinkers are phenomenal strategists. Not only are they tuned into trends and patterns among those around them, they're always focused on creating their next big, inspired project. Both habits make for great preparation for the future. True creativity requires being able to see things differently from everyone else and to learn something new every day.

Creativity is faceted like a diamond and has wide-reaching dimensions in the modern marketplace across all industries. For those who have cultivated creativity all their lives, leadership should come more naturally these days than ever if it's recognized, unearthed, and harnessed.

QUESTIONS FOR YOU:

1. Do you crave dominance and control? Do you hold a position of natural influence?
2. Are you attracted to or in conflict with the idea of compliance? What is your state of steadiness? Is it situational or constant? Are you a reliable source of steadiness for others?
3. What is your state of connectedness with your team, staff, organization, or groups in general?
4. How comfortable are you with forecasting and designing the future?
5. How do you perceive your own sensitivity? Does it extend beyond the emotional to how they perceive their environment, sense of touch, smell, and taste? What is your sense of self? Do you feel able to know yourself, both limitations and strengths?

CHAPTER 9

YOUR CREATIVE TYPE

One of the most concerning and prevalent myths I encounter in my business every day is this: once a leader has achieved success and reached the level he/she wants to reach, they are surrounded by people ready to help, they know what to do, and they are protected from fear. And that every top leader is somehow cut from similar cloth made of skills sets and education and opportunity, and that the gregarious and driven will inevitably reach the top, come what may. However, some of the most isolated, lonely, desperate, and scared leaders I know are the top-achievers and creative people. They feel the pressure of a big job with a big company or the force of nature that is the name they were supposed to carve out for themselves in the annals of business history following an expensive education and a big leap to a top job.

Many leaders feel surpassed by those who work for them, particularly when they are empathetic and aware and give their high-performing staff opportunities for personal and professional growth at the expense of the company. They may feel the stretch of that employee outgrowing some of their progress, but they as the leader may have too demanding a schedule to actualize time for development, creative expansion, or even simple vacation time. More than anything else, many top-level leaders get mummified in red tape, so lost in the bureaucratic noise and the requirements of keeping a company liquid, growing, and achieving that they cease to be inspired.

Current and continuing research shows us that creative people feel more fulfilled at work, more balanced, more satisfied, and show much lower levels of stress. We know that highly successful and cohesive teams show vulnerability, support each other on a personal level, and offer safety and respect to each other in conversation and professional discourse. If today's CEOs are constantly on a plane or bogged down by recalls, regulatory, or the most recent drop in market share, are they engaging in any of the things they put in place to make their staff happy? No wonder CEOs don't typically consider themselves creative - where can they find the time? And when their teams often don't feel that creativity is being supported organizationally there's no pattern to practice as a group. Instead, there's the paralyzing fear of taking a risk putting creativity on the business agenda and being criticized for not putting fundamental business first.

I believe that everyone possesses this intoxicating creative heart which drives all of the passion, fire, and belief in their soul and that the closer the heart and their work are to each other, the more the person will feel at home in their own skin, feel patient with their nature and even their damage, and come to balance in their pursuit of supporting the same feelings for those who work for them, work with them, and love them. From today's research, we know that creativity and creative leadership only truly penetrate an organization and their audience when that practice begins and is modeled by the leader, continues by being translated to management, is applied with departmental teams and staff, is finally introduced to the audience in a new way with brand, positioning, and marketplace attraction.

I am not an organizational psychologist or a research psychologist, but my colleague and friend Andy Johnson is. He's not only extremely educated and wise about the creation of forms of assessment that will result in statistically accurate results, he's also very smart about the heart and one of the most creative, connected, and innately sensitive and perceptive people I have had the pleasure to know. This assessment is something Andy and I came up with quickly so that you can have a little perspective about where your creative gifts lie.

'HAPPY HOUR' CREATIVE TYPES SURVEY:

Welcome to the Creative Types Survey. Circle the statements that feel true and measure them according to the scale offered, then read the key and reflect on what creative type (or types) you are. Next to each of the numbered statements, score the statements using the following scale. Add up your scores to see what your total for that creative type is. You may score equally for several different creative types.

1 = strongly disagree; 2 = disagree; 3 = neutral; 4 = agree; 5 = strongly agree

THE INVENTOR

I've always been good at creating or developing better ways of doing things or ways to improve processes or tools.

_____ When I was a child, I was good at creating innovative ways to play with my toys or to solve problems.

_____Other people have told me that I'm good at inventing unique solutions to problems or tools to solve them.

_____I readily see how things we have now could be used in different ways or combined with each other to form better tools.

_____I have an ability to envision things that don't yet exist with great clarity.

INVENTOR TOTAL: _____

THE ARTIST

I've always been good at drawing, painting, sculpting, or other forms of artistic expression.

_____In grade school, other children saw me as a good artist (drawing, painting, or other artistic expressions).

_____People tell me that they think I'm gifted artistically.

_____My art work has moved or impacted people.

_____I need to have an artistic outlet to draw, paint, etc. If not, the desire to be creative builds up inside me.

ARTIST TOTAL: _____

THE THINKER

_____I've always been a deep thinker and able to synthesize thoughts and ideas.

_____I have conceived of ideas, models, or thoughts that I believe are unique to me.

_____When I was a child, I thought deeply about things in a way that was different from many of my peers or siblings.

_____I inherently see connections between models, theories, and ideas.

_____Other people have told me that I have unique or deep insights.

THINKER TOTAL: _____

THE ENTREPRENEUR

_____I'm gifted with identifying new business opportunities in the world around me.

_____When I was a child, I developed creative ways to earn money or to accomplish significant tasks.

_____People have told me that I'm good at monetizing the value related to products or services.

_____I tend to be an out-of-the-box thinker related to business opportunities.

_____I love the challenge of starting new business ventures; it feeds my need for creativity.

ENTREPRENEUR TOTAL: _____

THE MOVER

_____I'm very in touch with my body and movement.

_____Sometimes I need to act things out with my body to make sense of things.

_____I've had other people tell me I'm gifted at athletics, dance, or similar bodily activities.

_____When I was a child, I had better control of my body than most kids around me.

_____I have extraordinary abilities to use my body to express myself.

MOVER TOTAL: _____

THE ARCHITECT

_____I see spatial relationships easily in a way most people can't.

_____I have ability to see both form and beauty and functionality simultaneously; these two things easily connect for me.

_____When I was a child, I was gifted at creating unique ways to build things with my toys.

_____Other people have told me that I'm gifted at creating architectural, industrial, or similar kinds of three-dimensional design that is useful.

_____I have the ability to envision how people will use the spaces or objects I design to make their lives better.

ARCHITECT TOTAL: _____

THE POET

_____I've had other people tell me I'm gifted at writing.

_____I've seen things that I've written move other people.

_____I have natural gifting in turning phrases and writing prose or poetry.

_____I'm quick on my feet verbally and often say witty, pithy or brilliant things.

_____I have always had the ability to create parodies of current songs on the radio on the fly.

POET TOTAL: _____

THE ACTOR

_____I have an uncanny ability to pretend to be someone else.

_____When I was a child, I could readily imitate many people around me or celebrities in the media.

_____Other people have told me that I'm good at drama, acting, or similar kings of activities.

_____I have been cast in plays or performances, beating out other people who have tried out for roles.

_____I have successfully performed in dramatic performances that have been moving experiences to the audience.

_ACTOR TOTAL: _____

THE MUSICIAN

_____I have natural talent in writing, creating, or arranging music.

_____Other people have told me I am gifted in using my voice or instruments in a unique way.

_____I connect in a very deep way with music and think about how it goes together or is constructed.

_____When I was a child, I had innate musical curiosity and an ability to play around with musical notes.

_____I think of potential melodies or lyrics or both in my head often.

_MUSICIAN TOTAL: _____

THE CONNECTOR

_____I feel deep empathic connections with other people and can sense what they are feeling.

_____When I was a child, I was emotional, had very close relationships with some people, and felt things very deeply.

_____Other people have told me that I am gifted at connecting with them.

_____I instinctively feel what other people are feeling.

_____I'm able to use my insights into other people to help them better connect to others.

CONNECTOR TOTAL: _____

KEY OF CREATIVE TYPES:

The following are general characteristics of the creative types. Calibrate your scores and compare against descriptions to see which are your most prevalent creative traits. Bear in mind that being the highest at something isn't the goal - creativity comes in all forms and scales, and the important factor is noticing where you gravitate and practicing/utilizing those traits as much as possible.

THE INVENTOR - Where problems find solutions

Designs things from scratch
Brewers
Winemakers
Distillers
Chemists
Engineers
Programmers / IT
Chief Operating Officers

THE ARTIST - Where beauty finds expression

Painter
Fine artists
Sculptors
Makers
Graphic designers
Web developers

UX developers
Chief Creative Officers

THE THINKER - Where thoughts merge with meaning
Thought leaders
Philosophers
Politicians

THE ENTREPRENEUR - Where value joins vision
Product designers
Authors of intellectual property
Creators of start ups
Founders
Chief Executive Officers

THE DANCER - Where movement translates meaning
Classical dancers
Yoga teachers
Barre teachers
Movement experts
Pilates instructors
Athletes
Massage therapists
Public speakers
Stuntmen

THE ARCHITECT - Where form means function
Industrial designers

Interior designers
Architects
Mechanical designers
Prop masters

THE POET - Where words translate life
Poets
Writers
Public speakers

THE ACTOR - Where imagination joins reality
Teachers
Actors
Performance artists

THE MUSICIAN - Where sound locates method
Songwriters
Composers
Lyricists
Rhythmists

THE CONNECTOR - Where emotion meets connection
Therapists
School counselors
Psychologists
Executive coaches
Acupuncturists
Alternative medical experts

QUESTIONS FOR YOU:

1. What do you do that nurtures your creative type or types? What can you do more of?
2. What creative types that are different from you might be most supportive for you? How could you enhance each other's work?
3. Do you feel balanced in your life and/or work? Would creative expansion make you feel more balance?
4. How do you use color in your daily work? Name 3 ways that color could help you elevate your creative type if you integrated it into your workplace?
5. Do you carry or wear totems or messages that remind you of things you need to remember? How might this remind you to ground yourself and be present with creativity, and to give it weight and significance in your life? This could be an item of clothing, a piece (or pieces) of jewelry, or even a scent depending on what you connect to.

CHAPTER 10

CREATIVE SUPPORT VS. CREATIVE PROHIBITION

For most of us, this concept of self-care before care for others is very difficult. It can feel self-serving, narcissistic, shallow, and like we might be misperceived as selfish. This often applies to how we feel about serving our self-expression and our creativity - it isn't valued universally enough in the world, so it can feel like we're being frivolous and eccentric and superficial.

What we are now understanding is that it is critically important that we service our own creative need on a deep and personal level and that we translate that fullness and satiety to the way that we view and assist with the creative process of others - specifically our teams, organizations, and our customers.

The same devotion we offer to others and our willingness to assist them with process, we must give to ourselves, our organizations, and our customer base. There is great and lasting value in approaching the marketplace with the innovation of personal connection, authenticity, and vulnerability.

This isn't an esoteric suggestion, but a very return-on-investment and business growth-related concept that underscores the risk we have today living in a very, very, fast moving and transparent world. It only takes one CEO who poaches lions or one high-ranking executive who makes an insensitive comment in a tweet or diminishes their working staff to tank a successful organization that is existing on a steady diet of customers gained from a beautiful hollow brand and an average marketplace penetration.

When our approach is open and vulnerable and real, from the CEO's personal leadership strategy to the last Instagram post made by a staff member, the audience begins to jive with the transparency; they adopt a sense of faith and trust, subscribe to an honesty and a safety that says "this brand won't do anything to hurt me or the ones I love" and which trusts that if the organization does screw up it will be recognized, rectified, and repaired with grace, truth, and the respect their audience deserves because the audience trusts them to admit the mistake, correct it, and move forward in a better way. By leaning into vulnerability and away from creative prohibition and the lies we tell ourselves about the risks of transparency and leaning into creative support and a process that transforms organizations from the top leader to the marketing message, we aren't selling items - we're winning real and lasting trust.

Psychologist William Glasser tells us that choice is our most important asset. We choose each and every thing that we do and that we are driven by our base needs to make good choices. The feeling that we are controlled externally breaks down our feeling of safety and peace and limits or destroys our ability to feel autonomy, mastery, and a sense of purpose. Glasser's theory states that external control and disconnection from our environment and our sense of choice leads to addiction, crime, violence, academic failure, and abuse.

When we are young, creative prohibition is a product of the way we are nurtured and the environment we choose or that is chosen for us. But the pattern of continuing creative prohibition is a choice. It's an active decision not to disrupt, not to disturb, not to be uncomfortable, and to metaphorically put the oxygen mask on everything except ourselves.

Now that you are beginning to know who you are, how you got here, and where you got stuck, how can you change your world?

QUESTIONS FOR YOU:

1. Are you criticizing or blaming yourself for not being creative enough? For not pursuing creativity early enough in life? For not matching up to a standard?
2. Are you designing encouraging creative patterns in your life, your workspace, your daily process, and the people you surround yourself with at work and in life?

3. Do you find yourself complaining and blaming the process or feeling like you cannot move ahead with a professional pursuit or path because you've run out of steam or innovative ideas?

4. Do you trust yourself creatively? Where does this trust stem from? What nourishes it and feeds it? How could it starve if you didn't feed it and what can you do to prevent that?

5. Do you punish creativity or creative ideas? Think about the last time someone brought an interruptive concept to a meeting. What feelings did that process and the "dissonant" idea bring up in you?

CHAPTER 11

CHANGING YOUR WORLD

Think about how much time effort and thought we put into individual leadership. We are always trying to improve ourselves, grow, expand, develop, and rise. In spite of this effort, we are still lacking leaders in major segments of the marketplace - particularly in specific age groups and vertical slices. We historically assume teamwork is natural and a given if every individual on the team is healthy, capable, and willing to play. That is flawed logic. Would you say that any two people who are equally committed to living in one city and being in a partnership should get married? Does it make sense to risk a restaurant's evening by putting servers in the kitchen and chefs on the floor? Do you want your CPA to be a free-thinker and a willing risk taker? The short answer is "no".

We put the right people in the right roles according to talent, strengths, and, at some level, joy, particularly in the interpersonal slice of that example—people who cannot work together, don't trust each other, have no chemistry, and barely have alignment of goals and mission will not succeed when trying to work in tandem.

In the past, team assignments have been that arbitrary and without guidance. Thanks to the leadership and research of some large companies, we're starting to see the flaws in that logic. We can see that everything we need to develop in individual leaders—openness, vulnerability, sanctuary from the demands of the rest of the company, and a safe place to explore the depth of an idea (the best and worst parts of it)—we also need to nurture in groups. Innovation is the language of creativity and is driven by ideation which comes from multiple minds in a cohesive and honest space. Ideation + vulnerability + safety = creative convergence.

When we start to see vulnerability, controlled error, correction, and liberation and the people within a team can truly break down the paradigms of what defines them with the rest of the company and the world, we can see an identity forming as a leader or as a specific sort of team member. With that cohesion and convergence, we begin to see role shifts and innovation that works and lasts because it's vetted in a stable, controlled environment. We break down gender, color, and behavioral stereotypes; we are just humans with worries and pain and flaws, working on a project together, sharing our lives and details with each other. Creativity is born and developed in that space where we are willing to be exposed. This is the adult version of sketching something one hundred and fifty times and ending up surrounded by wadded-up balls of paper and tears in our eyes before someone tells us that it's going to be okay and gives us a small revision which makes version one hundred and fifty-one **the one**.

The creative team. Safety. Ability to fail and to make mistakes. Room to work flexibly within structure set by management. The ability to innovate and develop truly revolutionary new products. Who does this?

Google did it. They "ended average" and "leaned in" on creativity as it relates to humans, psychology, safety, protecting, and positive management skills. They looked at the research and saw that the measures they were using to determine job growth, salary increases, and assignments had no empirical base that related to the bottom line. In 2004, Google executive Todd Carlisle collected more than 300 dimensions seen as "critical" to the job and ran test after test to see if there was any correlation to work product/success. Not one single variable correlated to positive work performance at Google. In 2009, Google launched an internal research project called "Project Oxygen". The premise of the study was that managers matter to the culture of an organization.

They identified three major pitfalls that all of their managers were facing:

1. They were having trouble making transition from worker to team leader.
2. They were lacking a consistent, creative approach to performance management and career development for their staff.
3. They spent too little time on managing and communicating personal leadership for their teams to be effective.

As a result of the study, Google implemented an eight-point plan to help managers expand their creative leadership, expand the creative leadership of their teams, and improve.

The eight consistent creative habits of highly effective managers were:

1. **COACHING:** They were good coaches. They paid attention and knew the particulars about each member of their team.
2. **EMPOWERMENT:** They knew their team's strengths and empowered their team without micro-managing.
3. **SHOWING INTEREST:** They expressed interest in employees' development, leadership expansion, success and well-being.
4. **PRODUCTIVITY:** By using personal leadership plans with their staff, they were productive and results-oriented.
5. **EMPATHY:** They were empathetic and thoughtful communicators and listened to their teams.
6. **EXPRESSION:** They helped their employees with personal expression and career development.
7. **CLARITY:** They had a clear vision and strategy for the team which involved the team's specific input and the willingness to pivot.
8. **CURIOSITY:** They were naturally curious and kept up on key technical skills so they could advise and mentor the team.

Carlisle began his research because Google culture had been built on letting people stand on their own and do their own work successfully on the progressive premise that managers typically had broader technical skill than those they supervised. That all changed with the studies they put into place and results they found. Google had created an internal culture that was bureaucracy-laden and which strangled creativity and individuality.

In 2012, Google took it a step further than the management initiatives with an internal study called "Project Aristotle". They studied hundreds of Google teams to figure out why some stumbled and others soared.

Researcher Julia Rozovsky moved from her work as a Harvard Researcher and, after graduating from Yale, was recruited to head up the "Aristotle" project at Google. Rozovsky's team started by reviewing 50 years of academic studies about teams. Was motivation a primary factor? Reward? She came up with a lot of the same results we hear from Daniel Pink; motivation did not increase with extrinsic reward. She looked at behavioral type, the social makeup of the group, the overlap of what they liked to do in their free time, and what their departmental goals were and where those overlapped. They found no common ground. They looked at gender balance and the length of time teams spent together and compared these with measures for success. Most upper-level management had previously assumed that if you put similar behavioral types together or if your group were friends outside of the workplace, the results were better. The data showed that neither moved the work in a significant direction.

As they continued to study the groups, they finally started noticing the qualities that the good teams shared. First, members of productive teams shared "air time", speaking roughly the same amount of time as each other. Second, members had good "social sensitivity" and were smart and accurate about using empathy for each other and relating to each other intuitively. When you put these qualities of communication together, they amounted to the team creating a space of psychological safety for each other; a group culture that was a safe haven for interpersonal risk-taking. This meant that they could safely experiment with their thinking and make progress instead of seeing inefficiencies and setbacks. When Rozovsky and her Google colleagues cross-referenced this trait with psychological studies, the pieces finally fell into place. Where teams had empathy and leaders who were even-keeled, consistent, and in-control, the team was successful. When leaders were emotionally volatile, the rest of the team was caught up trying to avoid a "crash" and didn't have the time and space to solve the problem at hand.

Though they found other important components, the most critical common ground for successful teams was this safe, consistent, open, creative space. In late 2014, Rozovsky and her team began to share the data with the 51,000 Google employees. A manager named Matt Sakaguchi came forward and took a personal interest in the data and the results. He wasn't a typical engineer but he was remarkably good at managing technical people and had been successful at Google for 10 years. He and his team began using an advanced survey created by the Aristotle team to judge their norms, then the team began to study the results. In exploring the idea of psychological safety, Matt Sakaguchi became comfortable enough to tell his teammates that he had Stage 4 cancer and that he had been battling it slowly for a decade at work at Google but that it had returned and was worrisome. Another colleague shared a similarly personal concern. The team opened up and realized they didn't want to check their lives at the door for work and that it probably wasn't good for their work to do so. The concept of psychological safety meant they could be themselves. Empathy, sensitivity, and a creative approach to problem-solving were empirically connected to what Google needed to shift for the bottom line.

In 2012, a pivotal *Vanity Fair* article called the decade when Microsoft ran on stack-ranking as a leadership measure a "lost era". By 2015, Google, Deloitte, and Microsoft had all modified or abandoned rank-based systems for individuals and adopted new practices for measurement and growth.

We want to be ourselves at work and in our lives. It's personified by the actions of brave entrepreneurs, naturally-interruptive creatives, and business owners like Paul Jarvis, Jason Zook, or Jessica Rolph but it shows up in subtle places too.

In a five-generation workplace and factoring in the safe, creative psychological space needed for teams to thrive, we have two paradigms at work here. The first is the literal aging out of generations and movement by age group in the workplace and what this means for their business. The second is the state of mind for the majority left working together and how they are dealing with the state of the world, major global shifts, and a vastly different consumer audience.

The generational perspective by teams is a state of mind more than a condition of work. Emerging leaders have vastly different needs than 40-something-year-old mothers who are breadwinners; and retiring leaders in their last act have vastly different concerns than college interns stepping into the workplace. Google defined the principles of successful teams empirically, with years of research, data collection, analysis and post-analysis, and literally proved that connected and in-touch managers with a hands-on approach, kindness, empathy, and vertical leadership amongst co-workers trump all other conditions in a successful team and workplace.

QUESTIONS FOR YOU:

1. Can you draw connections between our love for creativity and our state of conflict? Why do you think this happens?
2. Can you identify your own creative type and the creative type of at least one person close to you? If you have taken one of the behavioral assessments, can you map any of your behavioral qualities to your creative type and make connections/find synergies?
3. Can you begin a personal creative leadership strategy for yourself with both an "internal" model (for the defense of your own creative state), and an "external" model (to share your creative state with the rest of the world)?
4. Do you understand the definitions and structure of what makes a safe and whole creative team within an organization and some of the skills needed to guide that team?
5. Can you see the correlation between your personal creative leadership strategy and the whole creative team strategy and how to map that to an authentic approach for your consumer and the marketplace?

CHAPTER 12

CONCLUSIONS

I went into writing this book thinking that I was someone who was in touch with creativity, it's significance in every life, and its value in the modern business space. Creativity is truly a process and it grows and thrives with practice (and more and more and MORE practice). Our relationship with creativity is very personal and intimate and it's deeply rooted in our childhood experiences, our pain as adults, our battles with shame and guilt, and our connection with pleasure.

While writing this book, I discovered that I am just as guilty as anyone else at blocking myself and slamming face-first into the wall of creative prohibition. I recognized what I was doing in fighting the creative wave and I have recommitted myself to regular practice. I am the proud new owner of a travel watercolor set and mini watercolor block and that is what I am doing when I fly or wait in airports. Creating art. Exercising the muscle. Knowing I will throw a lot away but also knowing my mind will spin with clearer and more focused creative thinking the more often I am in that zone.

I hope that you now believe that you can be creative. Let me say that another way - I hope you now see that you are instinctively creative and feel willing to explore and grow in that. Meet yourself again through a creative lens. Take some time with it. Get to know your creative side or sides, and walk into a state of play as you do so. Creativity is fun, it's beautiful, it's shareable, and as we have seen, it truly can net results both for personal balance and business leadership.

You'll notice that I have made some **Your Notes** pages in the back of this book. Mark this book up. Turn down the corners and write all over the margins. Nothing is precious. And this is your guidebook —make it yours. Fill the back with your plan for how your life is going to change. Then believe what you write and everything WILL change.

Here are 'starters' to help you root and stay rooted in your true creativity:

1. **Nurture your relationship with creativity.** It's really closely connected to putting yourself first and rooting your soul. Dismiss and release your previous expectations about creativity and about yourself in a creative space and start with a clean slate. Return to that childlike impermanence and create something, wad it up, throw it away, create it again, tear that one up and throw it away, and repeat until you are where you want to be.

2. **Share your creativity with others.** It's nurturing and comforting and helpful. It removes boundaries and barriers between humans and maximizes our opportunity to be present and available to each other. It tears down walls and lets you be authentic, which magnetizes the authenticity in other people. Make sure you spend time with creative people - ideally people who are wildly creative in very different ways that you are. Spend some time with them ideating, and look at that think space as relaxation. Get excited about what is possible and whenever you can follow something through.

3. **Seriously consider and explore impact creativity has had on your life.** Then think about the things you might be able to accomplish if you enhanced your creative time and space. What new things might be possible if you not only expanded your perspective this way but teamed up with several other people who were doing the same thing?

4. **Divorce duplicity and embrace all creativity.** It's time to be honest with yourself. Make friends with all of your creative natures and tendencies - the really attractive ones and even those that might sometimes make you moody or anti-social. You are who you are and you'll be happier in a space of honesty and creative release.

5. **Set up a system for your creativity.** We are all different beasts so your system is likely to be personal and it has to be one that you will follow. Give it as much structure as you are comfortable with

and commit to it - make it a habit and a practice and adopt it into your life permanently. Soon it will be so second nature that you will forget it wasn't always wired into your being.

6. **Remember - creativity is a circle.** You reach an end only to come back to a beginning. Take a note, add a feather to your cap, and know you're bound to return to the beginning. Just return better, kinder, gentler, smarter, and more creative.

The one thing that hasn't changed across the landscape of my life, over decades, through a complex fabric of experience, across oceans and throughout this process?

One thing is true and always will be.

I HEART CREATIVITY.

For the People I Love

For my husband, Adam — infinitely patient, a relentless supporter, and a true artist who has emerged over the course of our relationship, bringing his creativity to his life's purpose, his parenting, and the daily manifestation of his heart's purpose and his life's work. He is a brave man amongst strong women which is sometimes a blessing but always a challenge.

For my oldest daughter Kaysen — who birthed a whole new version of me and chose me to be her mama; who walks around with her heart totally exposed and vulnerable, uses her voice to sing loudly and often, creates visions from mind to pen, and dances with her body and her soul. You love bigger and bolder than maybe anyone I know and you love me every minute of every day.

For my younger daughter Maisie — my baby and my sister, who chose me as her mama but is also my teacher and my guide, and one of the people I am here to help, and be helped by, the most. You are a natural-born warrior, fierce in your love and your defense. You're a protector and a fundamental creator, cerebral in every move, and unusually poignant in your eloquence and timing.

For Adrian Orme — my co-creator, my first best friend, the giver of my voice, and ever in the center of my creative heart. You are always missed, but never lost. You are the beginning and the end and with me all the way. I do all of this with you - today and always.

For the city of Edinburgh — and the people in it for breathing life back into me before I could disappear. For all of the people who were there with me and stood by me there and in all of the time that has followed.

For my parents, Kerry and Betsy Robinson — who made me precisely what I am and always supported my creative autonomy.

For my brother Seth — who named me a "Survivor of Many Things" and gave me an infinite gift in that title.

For Justin Foster — my mirror, my soul brother, my fellow alchemist. I owe a great deal of my growth to you and I will always see you for all of the things that you are.

For Lisa Fisher — my favorite survivor and my sister, the woman who showed me the resolve and how deep-down I needed to go to find this book and to rise to the surface with it in my hands. We continue to unfold the strangest, sweetest similarities in each other and I expect that never to end.

For Jessica Rolph — my sweet friend, the magnificent, humble and accomplished woman who called me a "warrior" and a "hero" and made space in a phenomenally busy life to extend gestures of goodness to me as a reminder that all was not lost; who continues to show up creatively in so many fundamental ways in her work, and who always includes me in her creative process.

For Melissa Nodzu — who has both understood and been baffled by me, but who has always seen me for who I am, for what I am, and for where I am on the journey. You have been my guardian and my defender, and allowed me to be strong and weak and equal in both.

For Shannon Reagan —who walked into adulthood with me and showed up as my friend, my sister, my confidante, my neighbor, and just when we started to lose sight of each other came to my rescue in my hour of need, making my pain her pain, helping me find a purpose for others in the journey, and making my victory over the darkness hers.

For Jodie (Bradbury) Baynes — who saw me more than 20 years ago for who I am and loved me in the midst of it, and who circles back to me in the gentlest and most precious ways over time. Our journey is just beginning.

For Susie Orme — my friend, my sister, my touchstone, who reaches a new plane every day, who scales extraordinary heights, and devotes herself to the good of others. I knew from a very long time ago that we were on a mission together.

For Susan Orme — a supremely brave mama and history keeper who freely gives the gift of support, protection, and love. I am so grateful for my time with you.

For Ryan Fitzgerald — who decades after we began reminds me that true friendships have second and third acts, timelessness, and purpose in seemingly simple details.

For Nicola Biscardo — my brother separated by oceans - one of my favorite people to dream and create with. Who helped me create a library of tastes and scents and memories, and I can never be grateful enough. And for Francesca, who is opening our family's hearts over miles and time.

For Jeff Reynolds — for being a fast and fierce friend, and who gave me the dignity and support I needed and let me return to business-as-usual at my own pace.

For Tami Thorne —for giving me back my voice, restoring my faith in myself, helping me map my resilience, and for granting me access to the hidden reserve of strength it takes to be in this process and stand up to the evil and injustice in the world.

For Jean Fisher — who swooped in and saved the day at a critical time and who is giving me the opportunity to have a voice and to help others.

For Detective Paul Jagosh — for uncommon sensitivity and heart and for saving several parts of this book from destruction and returning them to me.

For all of my family—born and chosen— you know how much you mean to me because I tell and you and you give that back to me in measure; for that I am both proud and grateful.

About The Author

COURTNEY FEIDER, CPBA, CPMA, NCTMB is an Executive Coach and Organizational Brand Strategist who helps business leaders and brands draw new lines around their thinking and design the future. She utilizes her experience as an agency owner, corporate marketing executive, and serial entrepreneur to help leaders create advanced personal and organizational strategies in the face of change and interruption.

Working with enterprise and Fortune 500 companies, as well as small and medium businesses, she has done executive coaching, leadership training, brand strategy, communications and sales. Her clients have included Microsoft, Hewlett Packard, W Hotels, Whole Foods, Albertson's, Fred Meyer, Pfizer, Glaxo-Smith Kline, Merck, Astra Zeneca, Amgen, Dartmouth College, Beam Suntory, Oregon Tilth, The Oregon Wine Commission, Sundance Film Festival and many others.

Courtney Feider holds a Bachelors of Science in Community Health with focus areas, international study, and teaching endorsements in Marketing, Psychology, and Art. She is a Certified Massage Therapist and Aromatherapist with accreditation from the National Certification Board for Massage Therapy and Bodywork. Courtney is also a Certified Professional Behaviors Analyst, a Certified Professional Motivators Analyst, and an Advanced Applied Axiologist.

I Heart Creativity is Courtney's first book.

Working with Courtney

Courtney does executive advising and coaching, consulting, and speaking and can be contacted through her website, courtneyfeider.com. You can connect with Courtney on LinkedIn, Instagram, Facebook, and Twitter.

• • •

Your Notes

Your Notes

Your Notes

Your Notes

Your Notes

Your Notes

Your Notes

Your Notes

Your Notes

Your Notes

Made in the USA
Columbia, SC
29 August 2017